D0394204

Dinner at Miss Lady's

Miss Lady's house

Dinner at Miss Lady's

MEMORIES AND RECIPES FROM A SOUTHERN CHILDHOOD

by

Luann Landon

*Algonquin Books
of Chapel Hill*

1999

Published by
ALGONQUIN BOOKS OF CHAPEL HILL
Post Office Box 2225
Chapel Hill, North Carolina 27515-2225

a division of
Workman Publishing
708 Broadway
New York, New York 10003

©1999 by Luann Landon. All rights reserved.
Printed in the United States of America.
Published simultaneously in Canada by Thomas Allen & Son Limited.
Design by Anne Winslow.

Grateful acknowledgment is made to the following copyright holders, publishers, or representatives for permission to reprint recipes on the pages listed: Recipe on page 159 from *Cooking in a Castle,* © 1965 by William I. Kaufman. Reprinted by permission of Henry Holt and Company, Inc. Recipes on pages 54 and 194 from *More Gems* by The Garden Club of Georgia. © 1971 by The Garden Club of Georgia, Inc. Reprinted by permission. Recipes on pages 34, 78, 130, 135, 158, and 196 from *The Southern Cook Book* by Marion Lea Brown. Copyright © 1968, 1979 by the University of North Carolina Press. Used by permission of the publisher.

Library of Congress Cataloging-in-Publication Data
Landon, Luann, 1940–
Dinner at Miss Lady's : memories and recipes from a
Southern childhood / by Luann Landon.
p.   cm.
ISBN 1-56512-227-5
1. Cookery, American—Southern style.   2. Food habits—Southern States.
3. Evans, Mary Leila Copeland, 1887–1970.   I. Title.
TX715.2.S68L35   1999
641.5975—dc21   98-53264
CIP

10 9 8 7 6 5 4 3

*For my
husband, David,
and my mother,
Luann*

I would like to thank friends and relatives without whom I could not have brought this book to completion. Charlotte and Edgar de Bresson suggested I write the book, and my talented editor at Algonquin, Kathy Pories, helped me craft the final version. My thanks to many others for reading and tasting, for giving recipes, encouragement, and help with the manuscript: Elizabeth and Tony Harrigan, Elizabeth Hanson, Susan Van Riper, Penny Phillips, Panna Ansley, Leila Fowler, Alison Touster-Reed, Eva Touster, Luda Davies, Carolyn Newbern, Bob Sullivan, Janine and Jean-Pierre Limet, Claude and Vincenette Pichois, Mme. Georges Duby, Ruth and Francis Seton, Jo Church, Nancy Weatherwax, Jim Jones, Nancy Blackwelder, Leslie Richardson, Mildred Merritt, the late Catherine Booth, Wilma Tate, Cherry Clements, the late Mrs. Wayne J. Holman, Jr., and Louise Ware.

A Note on the Recipes

In writing about the South I knew as a child, I have used my memory *and* my imagination. This is the life I remember and want to remember. If, in some cases, I could not recall what food was served on a particular occasion, I created menus that would likely have been served. My grandmother's cook, Henretta, inspired my love of good food, but she never wrote down any of her recipes. Some of them were written down by my Aunt Virginia, who gave them to me. I have re-created Henretta's other recipes from memory, experimenting with each one until I achieved the authentic taste that I remember so well. Using those and other recipes handed down by grandmothers, aunts and great-aunts, and cousins, or occasionally given to me by friends or selected from my library of Southern cookbooks, I have attempted to create meals both reflective of that time and accessible to contemporary cooks.

L.L.

Contents

Dinner at Miss Lady's

Henretta and Aunt Virginia

INTRODUCTION

I WAS BORN IN Greensboro, Georgia, a small town eighty miles east of Atlanta, where my father's family had lived for a hundred and fifty years. In that small town, my family had a history. We had lived through, and lost, a war, and somehow, in the long run, we had won. We had inherited ways of doing things—speaking, writing, building, cooking.

In Greensboro there were three family houses. After we moved to Nashville, my sister and I spent our summers with our grandparents, Miss Lady and Judge, in Miss Lady's family home. We visited and played in the other two family houses—Cousin Eva's, across the street, and next door, the home of Miss Annie, Miss Lady's sister. The yards around these houses were full of magnolia, pecan, cedar, copper beech, mimosa, oak, and fruit trees; in the gardens grew lilies, gardenias, hydrangeas, roses, and camellias. Memories of my childhood are filled with wonderful cooking smells and the hush of shaded porches. It was a life that was whole — sensuous and unhurried, it had a certain feel, a characteristic taste.

My mother's mother, Murlo, was from "outside." After my father's death, she came to live with with us in Nashville and sometimes accompanied us to Greensboro. Murlo was an accomplished cook and made everything herself, unwilling to entrust her recipes to someone else's ignorance or carelessness. My father's mother, Miss Lady, was waited on by servants all her life and didn't even know how to make a cup of tea, but she had an infallible sense of how food should taste.

I hope my book will evoke an experience of life in the old South, as I knew it in my childhood, from family stories, posed sepia photographs preserved in albums, and velvet and silk clothes carefully packed in cedar chests. It was a life centered around the meals that took place in family dining rooms. The dining room was the heart of every old Southern home. Here the family gathered every day, gave thanks to the Lord for his blessings, talked of ancestors and descendants, weddings and christenings, gardens and fields. Life that had happened and life that might happen. Time passed sweetly and unhurriedly. We liked to think that we honored the past, celebrated the present, and took courage for the future.

Unlike most members of my generation, I grew up with old people. My family lived in small Southern towns or the old neighborhoods of cities in a time when the majority of the population had relocated to the suburbs. The older people in my family, not only grandparents but also aunts and uncles, great-aunts and great-uncles, and first and second cousins, either lived with us or came to stay for long visits, and they were very much engaged in our up-bringing. They taught me the things that they had been taught and thought important to pass on. Perhaps the most important thing they taught me was the significance of "good taste" in all its forms.

Now that I look back on that time, it seems to me that taste was the most important thing in our lives—certainly of the utmost importance to my grand-mothers who brought me up. Murlo and Miss Lady were Victorian Southern women. They expected me to have good manners, to behave well. But they also taught me how to season with just the smallest amount of salt added to the sweet, just the right amount of vanilla or rosewater or brandy; how to bal-ance the wings of a flower arrangement and set a table; how the textures of fine materials should feel; which colors go together harmoniously.

I remember spending long afternoons looking at Miss Lady's art books filled with color reproductions of European paintings. I loved the rich and subtle colors and shapes and the finery of the women's clothes. My sister, Susan, and I would dress up in the old things stored in the upstairs closets and cedar chests—we'd try on our great-grandmother's shifts, lace-trimmed and finely tucked petticoats, and trousseau dresses, or we'd slip into Miss Lady's old evening dresses. We would find an old ivory and lace fan or a fad-ing silk rose and practice posing, pretending we lived in the world of Van Dyke or Gainsborough.

Food was very important in our world. Murlo insisted on using fresh ingre-dients and making everything herself without taking shortcuts. She would get up very early every morning (after three or four hours of sleep—she spent most of the night reading) and make freshly squeezed orange juice, hot oatmeal with brown sugar and milk, and whole-wheat toast. Breakfast at Miss Lady's house, always prepared by Henretta, consisted of toast made from light bread, grits swimming in butter, scrambled eggs, bacon, and homemade preserves. There was a running controversy between Murlo and Miss Lady: breakfast in Greensboro was pure self-indulgence, like Miss Lady herself, whereas Murlo's breakfast was sensible, "good for you."

Murlo was almost six feet tall, slender and straight. She wore her long white hair in a bun pinned with old-fashioned hairpins at the back of her neck. Although I know that she did not always wear black, that's nevertheless how I remember her—in a long black dress with a jabot of old lace pinned at her throat with a cameo. She deliberately cultivated what she called the "standards" of her family and its past. Her father, a judge and plantation owner and a colonel in the Confederate Army, served as secretary of state of Arkansas in the 1890s. Murlo, born in 1874, brought up eleven brothers and sisters and ran her father's plantation when times were hard after Reconstruction. Her mother, pleasure-loving and indolent (a great deal like Miss Lady, in fact), couldn't be bothered with small children. She spent her time accompanying herself on the pianoforte, singing songs fashionable in London and Paris, dressing up in prewar finery, and playing parlor games.

Murlo nursed family and servants through hard illnesses (she lost her favorite younger brother in a typhoid epidemic), sewed clothes for the women and children, upholstered furniture, made curtains, darned socks, mended sheets and table linens, and preserved fruits and vegetables for the winter months. Her mammy (who had stayed with the family after the slaves were freed), Siney, named for Mount Sinai in the Bible, taught her to cook, and her mother must have taught her how to flavor a Charlotte Russe or a syllabub. I remember Murlo saying that people in *her* family were healthy (as opposed to Miss Lady and her relatives, who had delicate nerves and touchy stomachs) because they had been raised on virgin land: Arkansas, when her father settled there shortly before the Civil War, was new territory. The land had never been cultivated, and the fruits and vegetables grown there were prime specimens. All those vitamins, all those minerals went into our blood and bones, Murlo would say.

Unlike most women of her generation, Murlo was college-educated. Before she married she was principal of a school for the blind in Little Rock. She read me many children's classics, passages from Shakespeare, the Bible, and Bulfinch's mythology. She taught me to read and write when I was four. She insisted I start learning French in the first grade.

Murlo's taste was deliberately old-fashioned; her hard life had made her somewhat rigid and wary, and she condemned most modern things as "vulgar." But in the life she created around herself she captured a certain lyricism of the past. She once made me a dress of peach-colored silk, trimmed with old Alençon lace, shirring, and embroidery, with a belt of braided blue and ivory satin ribbons. My mother didn't want me to wear it because other little girls my age weren't dressed that way. But I liked wearing that dress. I could see that it was beautiful.

MISS LADY WAS barely five feet tall, with tiny hands and feet, and wrists so delicate that they gave under the weight of the family Bible. She was petted and indulged all her life by her strong and successful father. He created a life of softness and luxury for her that she became utterly dependent upon. She did not have working muscles, a strong back, or steady nerves. All her life force was concentrated in sensibility. If Miss Lady had lost her means of support and been obliged to apply for a job at Woolworth's, she would have melted down into a puddle of tears and disappeared through the cracks in the sidewalk. She never left her house except in her chauffeur-driven car; she wouldn't think of walking uptown. If she wanted to buy a dress or a hat, the shop sent over a selection. Her groceries were delivered. Mary Nell came from the beauty parlor and did her hair in her bathroom.

Home to Miss Lady was the Victorian house she had inherited from her father and the gardens around it, which covered half a city block. I can still see it so clearly: The front lawn that was so green and soft I was reluctant to step on it (flagstones that led from the street to the front of the house were placed so far apart that I was obliged to leap from stone to stone). The two-hundred-year-old oak tree that stood near the street. The magnolia in the side yard that Miss Lady had planted the day I was born. The cutting gardens running alongside the white fence. The barn, no longer used except as a storage place for old furniture, discarded paintings in magnificent gilt frames, and trunks of our ancestors' clothes, sewn with elaborate, graceful details. The old white clapboard ice house, built over a deep pit in the earth that had been filled with blocks of ice in the summer to cool the butter, milk, and cream, and where my grandfather cured his country hams. If I opened the door on a hot day, a foul odor rushed out of the dark interior, mingling with the smells of magnolia and roses from the nearby garden. Henretta's house: one room with a quilt-covered bed, a rocking chair, a fireplace, and a small bathroom. An aisle of mimosa trees that led from the back of the house down the terraces, parallel to the rose garden.

The early Victorian house next door was where Miss Lady's sister, Miss Annie, lived. My grandparents also kept up the antebellum house across the street as a home for Cousin Eva, my godmother, an elderly, unmarried lady. Beside it stood the Methodist church that Miss Lady's father had built in 1912.

But home to Miss Lady was the entire town of Greensboro—the uptown stores with their Victorian facades, the general store, which sold chicken feed, yard goods, licorice candy, and steaks, the bank my family owned, the two drugstores on opposite corners of the main intersection, where you could get real chocolate and cherry sodas and "orange dope" (Coca-Cola laced with orange syrup). There was the antebellum courthouse, red brick with huge white columns, where the old men of the town sat in rocking chairs on the front porch and talked their lives away. And the houses along the tree-lined streets (many of them belonging to Miss Lady's friends, related to us so distantly no one except Miss Lady was quite sure how): white clapboard with wide sprawling porches, some of them sagging and peeling beneath the boughs of the great magnolias that stood in their yards.

And the Greensboro cemetery that lay on the edge of town. Miss Lady cared for the family plot tenderly, making sure that, even in death, her ancestors were still "at home." Every Sunday afternoon at four o'clock, the chauffeur, LeRoy, would bring the old Buick around to the back door of the house. Henretta would climb into the backseat and balance a vase of freshly cut flowers on her knees. Susan and I would settle down beside Henretta, and Miss Lady would be helped into the front seat by LeRoy. After a bumpy ride through back streets, the car would move slowly down the cemetery's rutted red clay road and come to a stop finally at the family plot.

An ancient magnolia grew to one side but gave no shade to the graves, which turned unshielded faces to the hot Georgia sun. Henretta would take the rake and watering can out of the trunk, water the ivy growing on Edward Copeland's grave, place the vase of flowers against Leila Davis's headstone, polish the Carrara marble and the Georgia granite with a soft cloth, and then rake the white sand between the gravestones into wavelike swirls.

Miss Lady would walk slowly through the plot, linger before each grave, bend to pick up a leaf that Henretta had missed, adjust the peonies and the Queen Anne's lace in the vase, relate some incident from the life of great-uncle Hugh, and tell us to remember. Then she would pause before the small gravestone of her older brother, take her handkerchief out of her sleeve, and begin to weep quietly. He had died when he was two years old, before Miss Lady was born. Susan would whisper to me, "But she never even knew him. How can she be crying about him?"

LeRoy and Henretta would help Miss Lady back into the car, almost lifting her up and carrying her, as if they knew that her grief nearly paralyzed her. Susan and I would sit very still in the back seat listening to Miss Lady's sniffling, too young to understand such grief, too old not to be aware of it. We were always held in check by Henretta's and LeRoy's solemnity. LeRoy would slowly maneuver the car out of the cemetery, back along the shaded streets to the house, trying to avoid every bump that would jolt Miss Lady. Henretta would shake her head and say softly, "Miss Lady just can't take the rough world."

When Miss Lady was twenty-four, her father took her on an extended trip out West. On the train she met an eligible young man from New York who was taken with her and proposed. But Miss Lady refused him. She returned to Greensboro and married a distant cousin she had grown up with. I am not sure when people started calling my grandfather Judge. Certainly not at the time of his marriage to Miss Lady. A photograph of him from this period shows a rather ethereal-looking young man with a sensitive mouth and a high forehead. But I remember him as a very tall, stooped old man who would break suddenly into laughter when he was telling a story or playing with one of us. He passed judgment on all matters, large and small, and there was an un-spoken agreement among everyone in the family and Greensboro that Judge was always right. He claimed to be descended from George Washington's fam-ily and said proudly that he had very little education: "Only went through the third grade." I believe Judge thought that education was middle class, that a real country gentleman knew everything there was to know about hunting and fishing, the best tailors in Bond Street, and the best restaurants in New Or-leans but had no time for literature or music or painting. A connoisseur of lux-ury, Judge (who worked as an adjustor for a fire insurance company) once spent the equivalent of a year's salary in one week at a London tailor.

Together, Miss Lady and Judge lived an easy, pleasant life. Miss Lady bought antique furniture, silver, and old porcelain on her travels abroad, and her home became a work of art that she created all her life. Every corner of her house presented some tableau of soft colors and graceful shapes. The house was formal without being stiff, and its luxury had a certain dignity or, one might almost say, discipline. She intended her beautiful things to be handed down for generations to come. When I was just a child, she would take me by the hand and lead me into the parlor, pointing out the pair of white porcelain and gold leaf Vieux Paris vases on the mantelpiece, one painted with spring flowers, the other with summer flowers. "You will inherit these," she would say, "and your children after you."

Both Miss Lady and Murlo took scrupulous care of their "beautiful things." I was under the impression when I was a child that a Dresden vase was something of cosmic importance—and perhaps, after all, it is. But Murlo resented Miss Lady's capacity to buy almost anything she wanted, to indulge her taste for beauty and luxury. Murlo would turn an old dress, refurbish it with a piece of Alençon from her collection of antique lace, and wear it proudly to the dinner table in Greensboro, as if to say "My family was rich *before* the Civil War."

The most important word in Murlo's vocabulary was *family*. Her cooking, her sewing, her cleaning, her antique furniture, her severity, her sacrifices— all were for her family. Murlo would sometimes accompany Susan and me to Greensboro for the summer, to supervise our upbringing; she could not entrust such an important project to Miss Lady's unreliable sensibility. Packing to go to Greensboro was an undertaking Murlo took very seriously. We would have to make many appearances—Sundays at church, parties, trips to Atlanta, calls on Miss Lady and Judge's relatives and friends. White gloves, little crocheted handbags, smocked blouses, ruffled pinafores—Murlo worked for days to bring our clothes to that peak of starch and shapeliness that would melt so quickly in the Georgia heat. My mother, a Westerner at heart (she'd been raised in Kansas) who would have spent her life in jeans and tennis shoes if Murlo had let her, could only feign an interest in these proceedings.

She acknowledged, with a mixture of pride and regret, that her daughters were being brought up in the tradition of the old South, where being a woman meant being a work of art.

B A C K   T H E N,   L I F E seemed to have a sensuous quality that was so gratifying we did not feel the need to exist provisionally, to block out the present in favor of some hoped-for future that would make us alive and happy. Food had something of a sacred function in Greensboro. It was not just something that assuaged our hunger while we concentrated on something else, but was a reality that lived in every moment it was prepared and eaten. It was so good that we not only noticed it but were completely engaged in its presence. And it had a way of reconciling the dissonances and disorders in our lives.

The high point of every day was midday dinner. Dinner was at one o'clock, supper at seven. We always ate in the dining room, which was the most beautiful room in the house. Above the white paneled wainscotting the wallpaper design was of red roses on trellises. The leafy flowering branches seemed to intertwine in a thousand different ways, so that you had to look very closely to see where the pattern repeated itself. A large eighteenth-century brass chandelier hung from the high, white paneled ceiling. On most summer days at midday the light from the garden outside passed over the porch and through the two tall windows, hung with red damask over white silk "glass curtains," at the east end of the room.

The long mahogany table was always set with white openwork mats, crocheted by Miss Lady, silver so old the initials and engravings were almost worn away, and garden flowers. At every place was a glass of iced tea, Lipton's, the only tea available in Greensboro (Murlo ordered Darjeeling and Lapsang Souchong from New York). By the time Henretta transformed it with sugar, slices of lemon, mint, and melting chunks chipped from a big block of ice, it was a delicious golden drink, just the right accompaniment to her cooking.

Midday dinner in Greensboro is still vividly present to me. At one o'clock Henretta rings first the little brass dinner bell in the shape of a lady in a hoop skirt, and then the old black iron bell at the back door. We gather in the dining room, weaving together the individual threads of our mornings and our lives. We seat ourselves and Judge says grace. Typically, Miss Lady has had an attack of "nerves" and is dabbing at her eyes with her handkerchief. Murlo is exasperated with her for her lack of backbone. Judge is peeved because it might be necessary to call in Dr. Parker (who gives Miss Lady a sugar pill), and he could miss his fishing trip to the lake this afternoon. My mother's young and beautiful face is crossed with frowns—Susan, nine years old, will eat only grilled cheese sandwiches and Coca-Cola, and I, eleven years old, will eat only biscuits and dessert. She thinks of my father, who died three years before, after serving in World War II. She thinks of his beautiful hands, his elegant clothes, his wit. He was too sensitive to live, and now she must live for both of them. She has decided to spend only the summers in Greensboro, to live during the school year in Nashville. She must make a home for herself and her mother and her daughters, earn a living, pay the mortgage.

Aunt Virginia, my father's sister, has a sick child upstairs. Jimmie has whooping cough, and she is angry that the family chatter prevents her from hearing what is going on in his room. Her face is cross and flushed, but her voice is soft as she talks to Miss Lady. She is not really paying attention to anything happening outside her child's sickroom. Uncle Pete, Aunt Virginia's husband, can never forget that Miss Lady considers him a little bit common. His manners at the table become more aggressive than they really are because he must always prove that he is a plain man and proud of it.

Henretta sets the platters and bowls of food on the table. She passes the biscuits (small, short, and delicate, the best biscuits I will ever taste in my life) and Miss Lady says through her tears, "Take two and butter them while they are hot," as if taking two biscuits and buttering them while they are hot is an action likely to have tragic consequences. Murlo refuses to help herself to the stewed tomatoes. They have been cooked with bacon grease. For a long time. Too long. All the vitamins have been eliminated, and they have no nutritional value whatsoever.

Miss Lady tastes her chicken. Her face, for a moment serene with anticipation, crumples into disappointment, as if she had been looking forward to this chicken breast to harmonize her nerves and make the world right. "Henretta," she says, "I don't believe your chicken is as good today as it was last week."

"Is that so, Miss Lady?" Henretta says, her chin shooting out stubbornly. "That was a right young bird."

"It's a little tough," says Miss Lady. "I believe you overcooked it."

Susan and I look at each other. How could Miss Lady say such things? How could she hurt Henretta's feelings? Henretta who would die for her. I want to leap up from the table and throw my arms around her, say, "Don't cry,

Henretta, it's the best chicken I ever tasted." Henretta, great cook that she is, stands with dignity next to Judge's chair with the plate of biscuits in her worn hands, which are tender and pink on the insides and leathery and brown on the outsides. She is like an ancient statue that is being slowly worn away by bad weather.

Judge takes two biscuits, places them on his bread-and-butter plate, and begins to tell about one of the times he dined at Galatoire's in New Orleans. Again Susan and I look at each other. How can Judge be so insensitive? Doesn't he realize that Henretta's cooking is better than anything at Galatoire's? We look to Murlo for support. The expression on her face seems to say, "Just as I expected."

Slowly, Henretta clears the table. We listen to the sound of her shuffling carpet slippers, then the kitchen door swinging shut behind her.

Suddenly Miss Lady is crying in earnest. This morning, this time at the dinner table have been mere prelude to her real sorrow, her real despair. She is crying for everything, for the whole world. She is crying about tough fried chicken, about her little brother who died when he was two years old, about my father's death, about the gardenia bush killed by the frost in February.

Henretta brings in dessert. Carefully she places a bowl of blackberry-rhubarb cobbler in front of Miss Lady. "Try a little, Miss Lady. It'll do you good." She offers a cut-glass pitcher of cream on a silver tray. Miss Lady dabbles the cream over the cobbler and lifts her spoon as if it weighed ten pounds. She takes a bite. Slowly, as she savors and swallows it, the expression on her face changes. The light, buttery pastry, the sweet-tart fruit, the thick, dark red juice, faintly spicy—once again, Henretta's artistry has saved Miss Lady. Peevishness and self-indulgence give way to pleasure. "Yes," she seems to be saying, "I love all of you. Don't you understand that I want to give all of you beauty and pleasure and this world we live in contraries me? Won't let me? But now—but now—look what Henretta has done for us. She has created something perfect, out of bitter blackberries, sour rhubarb, raw flour, plain sugar. She's an artist as I am, only no one acknowledges us, no one knows how deeply we are wounded by ugliness, by unshapeliness, no one realizes how hard we work to mend the broken world."

The expression on Miss Lady's face is what Henretta wants, what she hopes for. The expression on Henretta's face is what I hope for. Her face breaks into the smile I love—her mouth, chin, cheeks, eyebrows, hairline— all, all warm, beautiful, heart-easing curves. The world is no longer flat; it is round. We will not fall off into uncharted darkness. We will go round and round on a path of life that will comfort and keep us.

Aunt Virginia takes a second helping of cobbler but foregoes the cream in deference to her diet—she is always trying to measure up to its rigors but never succeeds. She listens; not a sound from upstairs. Fannie, Jimmie's nurse, *is* reliable, even if she does let the child eat sugar directly out of the sugar bowl.

My mother is saying to herself, "Well, at least the girls *look* healthy—I must be doing something right." She smiles and I look at her and think that she is beautiful, though she doesn't have the sort of porcelain prettiness appreciated in Greensboro. Her beauty is more contemporary—wide, high cheekbones, a mouth that smiles generously, a broad forehead, frank and hospitable. Of course I don't recognize these qualities as being contemporary on this occasion, when I am eleven years old, but I do realize that my mother is different from my grandmothers—not etiquette, sensibility, and soul, but a forthright handshake, a brave heart, and no fuss.

Miss Lady says she will have a second helping of blackberry-rhubarb cobbler with just a drop of cream. Henretta's movements as she serves Miss Lady are springy and confident.

Murlo looks at Miss Lady and shakes her head. The bad blood must have come in from Miss Lady's father's line; her mother's line is definitely good. Mentally she compares Miss Lady's and Judge's genealogical charts with her own, as she has done hundreds of times. Yes, she must admit, the Evanses and the Fosters, her own family, are almost (not quite) evenly matched.

Uncle Pete leans away from the table, balances the delicate Victorian chair on its back legs, and says, "I'm about to pop." There is a brief silence as this word "pop," not quite in the tone of the occasion, seems to run around the table and slap our faces. Uncle Pete bumps his chair forward, gets up from the table, takes his leave without a word of appreciation to Henretta, and readies himself to walk two blocks back uptown to his drugstore. Before he leaves the house, Aunt Virginia follows him into the hall. We hear low voices as they tell each other good-bye. I remember that this morning as I passed their bedroom door, I saw them sleeping in each other's arms. After we hear the front door close, after we hear Aunt Virginia's footsteps, full of concentration and energy, running upstairs to her sick child, Miss Lady sighs and says, "Virginia and Pete *are* in love." I want her to say more, but of course she doesn't.

It's the time of day when it seems that the difficult morning has passed, and now the lovely, long afternoon waits. We came to the table hungry, cross, wayward, sorry we had been born. We leave with generous hearts, loving one another, not wanting to change places with anyone on earth.

Murlo with Luann and Susan

*A Golden
Cake,
a Green
Plate*

THE DAY OF my tenth birthday, Henretta filled Miss Lady's house with vases of flowering crabapple, wild plum, forsythia, japonica, and daffodils. Murlo spent the morning in the kitchen baking her angel food cake. Susan was allowed in, but I was not. Periodically, Susan raced upstairs, where I was bored and restless, to give me bulletins from the kitchen.

"Henretta burned the boiled custard," she said. When she saw my fallen face she said, "Well, not quite." Then, not content with her merciful gesture, she added, "Murlo says the cake might fall."

My mother and Henretta never showed any favoritism for either Susan or me, and to Henretta a child was a privileged being. That morning she had pressed our taffeta party dresses, made by Murlo, identical except that mine was green and Susan's was pink.

"Which is the best color, Henretta?" Susan asked.

Henretta arranged the dresses carefully on the hangers, fluffing the lace collars with her deft fingers, giving herself time to compose a diplomatic answer.

"Well, honey," she said, "green is mighty fine, but pink is superior. Now take these dresses upstairs and hang them in your closet *so they won't get crushed.*"

With a dress dangling from each outstretched arm, Susan tiptoed up-stairs—if she made a noise the dresses might develop wrinkles. Triumphantly, she entered my room and twirled around, swishing the skirts.

"Pink is superior!"

Murlo's and Miss Lady's naps after midday dinner seemed interminable. Finally, we heard Miss Lady go into the kitchen, seat herself at the table, and wait for Henretta to bring her cup of coffee and whipping cream. Susan leaned over the bannister and reported on movements downstairs.

"Miss Lady has woke up," she said.

"Miss Lady has awakened," I said. I had been reading *Idylls of the King,* and "woke up" sounded to me unbearably inelegant.

Murlo joined Miss Lady for her afternoon cup of tea. My mother looked at her watch—two-thirty—the ladies still had time to dress. She hurriedly tried to fix our hair (she didn't do it as well as Murlo), tie our sashes, and buckle the straps on our patent leather shoes. As for herself, she had put on a simple linen dress and run a comb through her short brown hair. She looked beauti-ful and had spent perhaps five minutes becoming so, in a household where considerable time and effort were considered necessary for getting dressed.

Susan and I stood in front of the dressing table mirror in my mother's room. Susan was delighted with what she saw. Her long blonde hair, tied with a pink ribbon, fell down her back. She danced over to the dressing table, pressed the tip of her nose against the mirror, and said, "I am *so* pretty!" My mother said, "Yes, you are pretty, darling. You both are," turning to me. As for myself, I wasn't so sure.

A vase of pink camellias stood on the dressing table. Their scentless petals seemed to be at once buttery soft and firm as marble, nestled among the shiny, black-green leaves. I took a large one from the vase and pinned it in my hair with my barette.

"Look what Luann has done to her hair!" Susan shrieked.

My mother gave me an appraising look. "You're ten years old, not twenty."

"Just the right finishing touch," said Susan, slipping a camellia beneath the ribbon in her hair.

Murlo entered the room, dressed in her long black silk dress fastened at the neck with a cameo. She immediately took stock of the situation.

"These children cannot wear flowers in their hair."

"Why not?"

"They're much too young."

Susan and I danced around in front of the mirror, smiling at ourselves and turning our heads to get the best angle.

"You are both going to turn out vain and selfish," said Murlo.

My mother replied calmly, "You have to love yourselves before you can love other people." For once Murlo, who always had an answer, had nothing to say.

At three o'clock, Miss Lady's sister, Miss Annie, arrived with her grand-children, William and Amy. Seven-year-old Amy, a beautiful girl with radiant red hair, looked like a porcelain figurine as long as she was standing still, but at the slightest stirring of life she broke into involuntary, uncoordinated movement. Susan had always complained that whenever she set the table for a doll tea party, Amy's uncontrollable elbows knocked the whole thing over.

Other children arrived, left at the front door by their mothers and nurses. We obediently gathered at the door of the dining room to admire the artistry of Henretta and Miss Lady. Yellow, blue, green, and pink balloons and streamers floated beneath the chandelier; favors and shiny paper hats decorated the table. At every seat a plate and bowl from Miss Lady's antique dessert service had been carefully placed, and in front of mine at the head of the table the angel food cake stood majestically on Leila Davis's green and gold porcelain cake stand. A large cut-glass pitcher held the boiled custard. I could see at Susan's end of the table Murlo's Dresden compote dish filled with chocolate candy. Murlo was immensely proud of that dish, painted with delicate spring flowers.

My mother looked over all this finery worriedly. Children, she thought, ought to be allowed to make a mess of things, to make all the mistakes they felt like making and were bound to make. They ought to have been eating off of paper plates and napkins. But for once Murlo and Miss Lady were in agreement: children must learn to use fine things. For Miss Lady's part, she loved other people in the way she wanted to be loved herself. The lavish table perhaps reflected a memory of *her* tenth birthday party. She wanted me, her favorite grandchild, to embrace the beauty she loved. And Murlo, with her teacher's instinct, wanted to instruct us in the right aesthetic, in good taste. Not to be outdone by Miss Lady, Murlo had contributed her most precious possession, her Dresden compote dish.

We settled into our chairs at the table. At my place, among smaller packages, sat a long silver box tied with a green ribbon. I knew that this was Miss Lady's present, and my mind filled with delicious fantasies. That long, slender box, covered in silver paper, tied with a pale green satin ribbon! But I knew that I could not open the best present first. I began opening the others. A red change purse from Amy. I thanked her and rushed on. A book about the Bobsey twins from William. A diary with a little gold key, a stuffed monkey. A children's book of classical myths from Murlo. Soon the gifts lay helterskelter on the table, and the floor around my chair was littered with wrapping paper and ribbons. Now only the silver box remained to be opened. My hands trembled.

"Go ahead, darling," Miss Lady said.

The green satin bow loosened at a touch from my fingers. I lifted the lid and carefully parted the frothy mass of tissue paper. Lying in her white bed was the most beautiful doll I had ever seen. I lifted her from the box and held her up so that I could see every detail of her perfection.

"My mother gave me that doll on my tenth birthday," said Miss Lady. "I sent it to a special place in Atlanta to have it refurbished."

Already I had decided who she was—Scarlett O'Hara as a little girl. Her bisque porcelain face was the color of a white peach, with the faintest blush on her cheeks. Her dark auburn hair, thick and long, fell into an opulence of ringlets, and her eyes were hazel, luminous glass with tiny black pupils and ivory lids that closed languidly. Her lashes were thick and black, stiff little brushes, and she wore a pale green organdy dress trimmed with white lace. Her body of white kidskin was stuffed with sawdust (Miss Lady said), and her tiny, unchipped hands and feet were of bisque porcelain. She wore white pantaloons, white silk stockings, and soft, cream-colored leather shoes with straps that fastened with gold buttons. On her head was a hat made of woven leaf-green straw and trimmed with floppy, pale green roses and leaves tucked into a delicate green veil.

"Show the doll to your guests," Murlo instructed me.

Slowly I turned the doll around so the other children could see her. Involuntary sighs escaped from Susan and Amy. Susan's face was sullen; there would be no such gift from Miss Lady on *her* tenth birthday.

"What is her name?" Amy asked.

"Scarlett," I said. A moment of respectful silence, as everyone agreed that she was well named.

I watched apprehensively as Henretta removed Scarlett and the other presents from the table and arranged them on the sideboard. She lit the ten yellow candles on the cake. "Make a wish! Make a wish!" shrieked Susan and Amy. Involuntarily I whispered, "Thank you," and blew the candles out. I didn't know whether I was thanking Miss Lady or God.

I tried to cut the cake as I had seen Murlo do it. She and Henretta handed round the plates and Henretta passed the custard. The cake was very moist and light. My mother, Miss Annie, Aunt Virginia, even Miss Lady, knowing how proud Murlo was of her cooking, were careful to compliment. A glimmer of pleasure passed over Murlo's stern face as she stood very straight and tall beside me, watching carefully to see if the children were eating her cake, if they were learning how fine food should taste.

Because it was a birthday, we were allowed to eat as much dessert as we wanted. We advanced into our second or third helpings. Amy, sitting at Susan's end of the table, eyed the chocolate candy in the Dresden compote. She bolted from her chair, reached across the table, and grabbed the compote by the stem. The delicate dish tottered and swayed, then suddenly crashed over on its side, the chocolates scattering across the table. The rim hit the silver dish filled with daffodils.

A hush fell over the room. Slowly, Murlo walked to the other end of the table. She bent over to pick up the compote dish. She held it up to the light. A large piece the shape of a half-moon was missing from the rim. Her straight figure swathed so bravely in black silk suddenly went slack. I did not have the courage to look at her face.

Amy burst into hysterical heaving sobs.

Murlo set the compote on the sideboard, beside my Scarlett doll. "We musn't cry over spilt milk," she said in a quavering voice. I prayed that Murlo would not cry. Murlo never cried.

"Henretta," Murlo said in a firmer voice, "I think you could offer the children one more piece of cake before they begin their games."

The conversation became awkward and subdued. "Mrs. Foster," said Miss Annie (only the children called her Murlo), "I would love to have your recipe for angel food cake. I've never tasted its equal." She said this hesitantly and lamely, as if trying to cure cancer with a Band-Aid.

Murlo answered with a regal nod of her head and drew herself up majestically to her full height. "I will copy out the recipe for you," she said to Miss Annie, "while the children are playing."

All of us were silent as she went into the kitchen, Henretta following behind her. Once the kitchen door had closed, we poured into the adjoining parlor to play musical chairs.

When I was left without a chair, I slipped into the dining room to see if Scarlett was still on the sideboard. Yes, she was there, sitting with her legs stretched out in front of her and her hands in her lap, leaning a little to one side. March sunlight poured in the dining-room windows, and in the kitchen Murlo sat at the table in her black dress, holding her back very straight and copying out the recipe, saying the words to herself as she wrote them down.

At five o'clock, the mothers and nurses returned to pick up their children. "Was it a wonderful party?" asked one mother.

"I busted something," said Amy.

"'Broke,' Amy, 'broke,'" said Miss Annie. Holding Murlo's recipe, she turned to Murlo. "I intend to make this myself." Like Miss Lady, Miss Annie had a cook. "I want to see just how such a—work of art—is put together. It's not often that Greensboro has a great chef in residence." Her voice trailed off, embarrassed.

The door closed behind all the guests, and Murlo excused herself. The shadows around her brown eyes, set deep in her face, were dark. Listlessly, she pressed her thin hand against her forehead. She had one of her headaches. She would go upstairs and rest before supper.

Quietly, Susan and I followed. "Let's go see her," said Susan.

"She doesn't want to talk to anyone," I said.

"She'll talk to me," said Susan.

Murlo's door was slightly ajar. We could see her lying in bed with the comforter pulled up under her chin, her arms by her side, her hands limp—

Murlo, who was always walking with her long, quick stride, bending over a mixing bowl, making a bed, weeding a garden, sewing, reading, writing letters.

Susan went quietly into the room and stood beside her bed. She touched Murlo's hand. Murlo opened her eyes.

"I want to try to sleep for a while. Run along, now."

As Susan turned to leave, Murlo reached out and took hold of her hand. "Breaking a beautiful thing," she said, "is like breaking off a piece of your heart."

My mother told me years later that what Murlo wanted most in life was to have enough money to live with ease. But when we were children, she wore her poverty so bravely that we never realized she was crushed by it. There was always ample good food on her table, and she offered to buy our school clothes and party dresses and to pay for piano and ballet lessons and any books we needed. Murlo's clothes were very old-fashioned, carefully brushed and mended, but we had thought that this was part of the style she deliberately cultivated.

Murlo closed her eyes. Susan tiptoed out of the room and shut the door quietly. We stood with our arms around each other, rocking back and forth.

THE NEXT AFTERNOON, Amy came over as if on a mission to find Susan and me. She kept her hands behind her back.

"I'll tell you something I bet you don't want to know," said Amy.

Of course we wanted to know. "I told you," said Amy, "you don't want to know."

"How come?" said Susan.

"It's something awful," said Amy. "Miss Annie made Murlo's angel food cake this morning. It turned out terrible. It looks like a rubber pancake. It tastes like old chewing gum."

Susan and I laughed. "Miss Annie doesn't know how to cook," Susan said.

"She does too know how to cook." Amy said that Grover, Miss Annie's cook, had looked at the recipe and said that he thought something was missing. She showed us a piece of paper she held crumpled in her hands. "This is the one Murlo copied out. We could get her recipe book and compare them."

The house was quiet. Henretta was working in the garden, Miss Lady and Murlo were taking their naps. Mamma had gone across the street to pay a call on Cousin Eva. There didn't seem to be any reason not to go into the kitchen and find the book in the pantry. I reached up to the top shelf, pulled it down, and laid it open on the kitchen table. Amy smoothed out her wrinkled paper. Turning the brittle yellow pages, we located "Angel Food Cake." Amy ran her finger down the page.

"Cream of tartar!" she shouted. "Murlo left out the cream of tartar!"

"So the cake didn't rise," I said.

"She did it on purpose," Amy said. "Murlo left it out on purpose!"

"She did not!" Susan said fiercely. "Murlo would never do such a thing."

"She did too!" said Amy. "And I'm going to take that flat thing to the church supper tomorrow night to show the whole town Murlo's famous angel food cake."

"You can't do that," Susan said.

"And why not, if she's mean enough to leave the main thing out of the recipe?"

"It was a mistake," said Susan.

"It was not," said Amy. "She was trying to get back at me, trying to tell every-one that I broke her dish—her horrid old dish—trying to tell everyone that I'm clumsy." Amy began to sob hysterically again. She ran frantically out of the kitchen and down the back porch steps, slamming the door behind her, and disappeared into the green depths of Miss Annie's yard.

Susan and I were both thinking the same thing. "Murlo would never—" said Susan. "Never," I said.

We went out onto the front porch and waited for my mother. We watched her say good-bye to Cousin Eva, cross the street, and walk across the lawn. She sat down beside us, and we told her about the cake. Susan asked if Murlo would do something like leave out the cream of tartar on purpose.

"People do mean things when they are angry or hurt," said my mother.

"But Murlo is so good," said Susan.

"Noble," I said.

"Murlo is good," said my mother. "When I was a little girl and we lived on a farm in Kansas—it was the Depression—no one had any money. No matter how many poor people came to the back door, Murlo always fed them. She never turned anyone away."

"So Murlo would never leave out the cream of tartar on purpose," said Susan.

"That's not what I'm saying," said my mother. "We'll never know whether she did or not."

"We'll ask her," said Susan.

"No, we can't do that. The thing to do is to tell her that Miss Annie's cake didn't turn out and that she wanted to take it to the church supper tomorrow evening."

Susan jumped up. "I'll tell her."

T H E N E X T M O R N I N G, Murlo was beating egg whites by hand when Susan and I came down for breakfast.

"Mrs. Foster," said Henretta, "I wish you'd use my electric mixer."

"Egg whites mount higher when they are beaten by hand," said Murlo.

"I don't know where you get your energy. I'd as soon chop wood as beat by hand."

"Henretta," said Murlo, "where is that imported vanilla?" Henretta fetched the bottle of vanilla extract from the pantry.

"I might have known Miss Annie couldn't make this cake turn out right," Murlo said. "She can't even boil water."

Later in the morning we returned to the kitchen to find the cake, tall and golden, sitting on the table.

Murlo said, "Sometimes when I've made something like this I just like to look at it. Walk around and observe from all angles. I know how the Lord felt when he put the last blade of grass in the Garden of Eden."

"Can we take it to Miss Annie?" Susan asked. Murlo hesitated.

"All right," said Murlo, "but don't drop it."

Susan reverently lifted the cake off the table, held it high. I followed her and triumphantly we proceeded out of the kitchen, down the back porch steps, through Miss Lady's side yard toward Miss Annie's house.

I knocked. We knew Grover would answer. Grover always answered Miss

Annie's front door; he was the mainstay of her family. Her husband had died when her children were young, and Grover had become their best friend and really their father. Now he was raising the grandchildren. When he was with children he gave them all of his attention. We knew that, like Henretta, he took us more seriously than anyone else did.

Grover opened the door. He was tall and thin, dressed in black trousers, a starched white coat, black bow tie, and immaculate white gloves. His face broke into a smile.

"Miss Luann and Miss Susan, I'm mighty glad to see you."

Susan thrust the cake into his hands.

"Murlo sends this cake to Miss Annie—" I said.

"And to Amy," Susan said.

"To Miss Annie and to Amy," I said, "for the church supper tonight."

"You tell Mrs. Foster that's a mighty fine cake. Miss Annie will be real proud to take that cake to the church supper."

"And tell Miss Annie and Amy," said Susan, "that Murlo sends them her kindest regards."

"I will certainly tell them," Grover said solemnly, "that Mrs. Foster sends her kindest regards."

Two days later, Grover appeared at our door and delivered a package to Henretta, which she carried in to Murlo.

"Grover has brought you a present from Miss Annie," she said to Murlo.

She handed Murlo something large and round, wrapped in tissue paper, with an envelope taped to the paper. Murlo took the package, balanced it with her hands, found it heavy. Carefully she unwrapped it and held it up for us to see: a large, pale green porcelain plate painted with an arabesque of green and purple grapes, rounded with leaves and tendrils. Murlo opened the envelope and read the note to herself. Then she read aloud:

Dear Mrs. Foster,

I probably don't need to tell you that your cake was the high point of the church supper Wednesday evening. A good cook cannot fail to know her own worth. I looked through my things, trying to find something to give you that would be adequate reciprocation. I want you to have this Limoges plate, decorated by my mother, Leila Davis. As you know, ladies painted porcelain in the old days and sometimes achieved a high degree of felicity. Imagining your golden cake on this green plate is to me a beautiful vision. I hope you will find it so too.

With kindest regards, Annie

Murlo held the plate up to the light, ran her fingers over the surface, examined the painting with her connoisseur's eye. She did not want us to see how pleased she was.

Menu I:

A dinner that measured up to Murlo's standards.

❧

Curry Soup
with Lemon and Sherry

Chicken
with Roquefort Sauce

Asparagus
with Lemon Dill Butter

Leslie's Southern French Bread

Murlo's Angel Food Cake
with Boiled Custard

Curry Soup with Lemon and Sherry

This chilled soup makes a nice first course. With French bread and a tossed salad, it can also be the centerpiece of a light lunch.

> 6 cups chicken broth, strained
> 6 whole eggs, beaten
> 4 tablespoons lemon juice
> ½ teaspoon salt
> ¼ teaspoon white pepper
> 3 tablespoons sherry
> 1 tablespoon curry powder
> fresh parsley, finely minced

1. Place the chicken broth in a medium saucepan and bring to slow boil.

2. In a large bowl, beat the eggs until frothy and add lemon juice. Slowly pour hot stock by cupfuls into the beaten eggs, stirring constantly. Add salt, pepper, sherry, and curry powder.

3. Cover and chill for several hours. Serve garnished with parsley.

8 servings

Chicken with Roquefort Sauce

*E*asy to make, this dish is fancy enough for company. It was inspired by a meal we ate at a wonderful restaurant in Louisville, Kentucky, The Old House.

> 1 cup flour
> 1 ½ teaspoons salt
> ½ teaspoon pepper
> 2 pounds (2 large) chicken breasts, halved, bone in
> 4 tablespoons butter
> ½ pound mushrooms, sliced
> 1 teaspoon chopped onion
> 1 medium tomato, peeled and chopped
> ½ cup dry white wine
> 1 cup heavy cream
> 1 cup (3 ounces) Roquefort cheese, crumbled
> fresh chopped parsley

1. In a large plastic bag, mix flour, salt, and pepper. Dip chicken breasts in flour and shake off excess.

2. Melt butter in a large skillet. Sauté chicken over medium-high heat until browned on all sides, about 6 minutes. Turn heat down to low, cover, and cook until chicken is tender, about 30 minutes.

3. Remove chicken from skillet and keep warm. To juices in pan add mushrooms, onion, tomato, and white wine. Cook briskly until most of the liquid has cooked away, about 5 minutes. Add the cream and the crumbled Roquefort cheese and cook very gently until cheese is melted. Correct the seasoning.

4. Place chicken on a heated platter, pour sauce over, and sprinkle with parsley.

4 servings

Asparagus with Lemon Dill Butter

A light vegetable dish to accompany the rich chicken.

> 2½ pounds fresh asparagus, trimmed of
>   tough bottom ends
> 3 tablespoons butter, melted
> juice of 1 lemon
> 3 tablespoons fresh chopped dill

1. In a large skillet, cover asparagus with cold salted water. Bring to boil, reduce heat, partially cover, and simmer until firm but tender, about 15–20 minutes. Drain and keep warm.

2. Add lemon juice and chopped dill to melted butter.

3. Arrange asparagus on a platter. Pour sauce over. Serve immediately.

8 servings

Leslie's Southern French Bread

A delicious bread which is very easy to make and can be frozen. It goes well with most of the menus in this book.

> 1½ tablespoons Crisco shortening
> 1½ tablespoons sugar
> 1 teaspoon salt
> 1 cup boiling water
> ½ cup milk, scalded
> 1 package dry yeast, dissolved in ½ cup warm water
> (105°–115°F)
> 4 cups flour

1. In a medium bowl, mix together shortening, sugar, salt, water, and milk. *Cool to lukewarm*, and add yeast mixture.

2. Measure out flour in a large bowl. Stir liquid mixture into flour. A soft dough should form. Do not knead.

3. Cover and let rise until double in volume, about 1 hour, or put in barely warm oven, covered, about 1 hour.

4. Turn out on floured board and knead lightly, using very little flour. Cut dough in half and shape into two long loaves. Place on a greased baking sheet. With sharp knife, cut diagonal slits across tops of loaves. Let rise *uncovered* until doubled in volume, about 1 hour.

5. Bake in preheated 400°F oven for 15 minutes; reduce heat to 350°F and bake about 15 minutes more.

30 slices

Murlo's Angel Food Cake with Boiled Custard

Nothing matches the simplicity and lightness of this classic cake.

12 egg whites from large eggs
1¼ cups sifted cake flour
1¾ cups sugar, divided
½ teaspoon salt
1½ teaspoons cream of tartar
1 teaspoon vanilla extract
½ teaspoon almond extract

1. In a large bowl, let egg whites warm to room temperature, about 1 hour.

2. Preheat oven to 375°F.

3. Sift flour with ¾ cup of the sugar, and resift 3 times. Set aside.

4. With electric mixer at high speed, beat egg whites with salt and cream of tartar until soft peaks form. Gradually beat in remaining sugar, beating well after each addition. Continue beating until stiff peaks form. With spatula, gently fold vanilla and almond extracts into egg whites until combined.

5. Sift flour mixture, ¼ cup at a time, over egg whites, gently folding in with a spatula. With spatula, gently push batter into ungreased nonstick 10-inch tube pan; smooth and make sure it touches sides of pan. With knife, cut straight down through batter twice. Bake on lower oven rack 35 to 40 minutes or until toothpick inserted in center comes out clean.

6. Invert pan on cake rack and let cool completely—about two hours—without removing cake from pan. Carefully loosen cake from pan by running thin knife around edges. Ice with Orange Icing and serve with Boiled Custard.

12 servings

Orange Icing

2 egg whites from large eggs
1 cup sugar
3 tablespoons Grand Marnier liqueur
¼ teaspoon cream of tartar

¼ teaspoon salt
1 tablespoon grated orange peel
3 drops yellow food coloring
  to make icing golden

1. In a medium bowl, combine all ingredients except orange peel and food coloring. With wire whisk (or hand-held electric mixer), beat about 1 minute to combine ingredients.

2. Transfer to top of double boiler. Cook over rapidly boiling water (water should not touch bottom of pan), beating constantly with whisk or mixer, about 7 minutes, or until stiff peaks form. Remove from water.

3. Add orange peel. Continue beating until frosting is thick enough to spread, about 2 minutes. Add food coloring.

4. When cool, frost cake.

2 cups of icing

Boiled Custard

This delicate custard may be served alone as a dessert.

12–14 egg yolks
⅓ cup sugar

2 cups light cream (half and half)
1 teaspoon vanilla extract

1. In a large bowl, beat egg yolks with electric mixer until thick and lemon-colored; gradually beat in sugar, then cream.

2. Transfer to saucepan and cook over low heat, stirring constantly with wooden spoon until the custard thickens (160°F on a candy thermometer). Add vanilla.

3. Cover and chill in refrigerator for one hour before serving.

12 servings

Henretta in her kitchen garden

Lightning Bugs

*F*ROM THE TIME our father died when I was eight and Susan was six, we spent every summer in Greensboro until we graduated from college and married. The town became a myth in our lives—that beautiful, warm Southern place where there was no work that had to be done or schedule that had to be met. All my memories of Greensboro seem to coalesce into a kind of long, fluttering ribbon, anchored in the present and stretching back into the past further than I can see.

The trip from Nashville to Greensboro was a long one. When we were children there were no interstate highways, so we took the old state roads. My mother drove us down, sometimes with Murlo, on the long Memorial Day weekend. Greensboro is one of several beautiful towns in the eastern central part of Georgia. Approaching each one, Susan and I were sure that *this* would be Greensboro. Then we would pass the white roadside sign with the name in dark green letters—Lithonia, Conyers, Covington, Rutledge, Madison—and we would have to admit that although this town was *like* Greensboro, it wasn't *really* Greensboro.

At last the red clay corn and cotton fields and the pine forests that lay between the towns gave way to little white frame houses, and the highway turned into Main Street. On the left on a hill rose Miss Celeste Smith's Victorian mansion, red brick with white gingerbread trim and a gazebo in the side yard. The car seemed to slow down of its own accord, as if to allow us to really see the huge white blooms of the magnolia trees that lined both sides of the street and the ebullient rose garden, with its big dainty flowers, in the McCommons's yard.

When we passed over the railroad tracks (I can still smell the tar on the wooden beams that formed the sides of the bridge) and saw on the right "the big house," Cousin Eva's, and on the left Miss Annie's, then finally Miss Lady's house, waiting peacefully for us, surrounded by its green lawn and old shade trees, white clapboard with rambling porches, red roof, green shutters, gables and bay windows, unchanged since Miss Lady's father built it in the 1880s— we knew we were in Greensboro.

Susan and I worried about the driveway. Winding around the house, lined with a low border of red brick over which grew carefully trimmed, shiny, dark green ivy, it was filled with fine, white sand that had been raked into wavy swirls. We thought it a shame to drive a car over that sand.

Miss Lady and Judge were always waiting for us on the front porch, sitting in their rocking chairs. As soon as we turned into the driveway they would stand up and wave to us from behind the porch railing. Miss Lady's face was a picture of relieved anxiety (she worried all during our trip that we would have a terrible wreck). We would drive round to the back of the house, where Henretta was waiting for us. And by the time we got out of the car, Judge and Miss Lady had come through the house and out the back door to join her. I never saw Miss Lady move quickly—she moved (and talked) so slowly—and I marveled that she could get through the house, down the back steps, and into the driveway, just in the time it took the car to round the corner of the house.

We always hugged Henretta first—she was our best beloved. She smelled wonderful—of peaches, flour, roses. Then Susan hugged Judge and I hugged Miss Lady, then the other way around. Miss Lady smelled of cologne and Judge smelled of tobacco.

Laughing, Henretta would say, "You're home now! Just help yourself!" She meant, "Just help yourself to all the flowers I've grown for you, all the peaches and pecans, all the ice cream and biscuits and cake I've made for you." Henretta's way of loving us was to pour upon us things that smelled and tasted good.

Judge carried our bags upstairs. The stairway curved up from the downstairs hall to the second floor, and there was a large stained-glass window on the landing, yellow, aquamarine, and rose, that let in the midday light. I remember the round newel post and the black bannister, which was smooth and cool beneath my hand. My steps seemed light and springy. At the far end of the upstairs hall, between the linen closets, was a bay window curtained in gray silk taffeta. There was a curved valance at the top, and the drapes were long enough to lie in voluminous folds on the floor. I thought this was true elegance.

My mother stayed in Aunt Virginia's room, to the right off the hall, and Susan and I stayed in the two bedrooms to the left off the hall. I always had my father's old room, at the front of the house, because I was the oldest grandchild and, I was told, just like my father. Susan had the adjoining room behind, filled with graceful country furniture and children's books. My room was high-ceilinged, decorated with green flowered chintz and old fruit and flower prints. Susan and I thought Daddy's matching carved furniture princely; in the chest of drawers there was a special cupboard for top hats. And there was always a red rose in a bud vase on the dressing tables in each of our rooms. Susan would run into her room to make sure that Miss Lady had not forgotten to give her one as well.

We all gathered in Miss Lady's and Judge's downstairs bedroom, which was also their sitting room. Judge sat in his big armchair; a piece of embroidered linen was pinned to the back so that his hair oil wouldn't stain the upholstery. Miss Lady settled into her rocking chair with blue ruffled cushions. She rocked and cried, cried and rocked. We were no more upset by her tears than by a baby crying. Miss Lady enjoyed all the glamour of being an adult and all the emotional indulgence of being a child. Every ten minutes or so, she excused herself to go to the bathroom. One time, after Miss Lady's fourth trip to the bathroom, Susan could not contain her curiosity.

"Miss Lady," she said, "I just don't understand how you hold so much water. All you do is cry and pee-pee."

Miss Lady was speechless. Susan was always saying unanswerable things. Miss Lady never knew what tone to take with her.

On this occasion, Miss Lady decided that her only possible response to

Susan's remark was to sink into her rocking chair and press her crumpled, scented linen and lace handkerchief against her forehead. Fortunately, Henretta appeared in the doorway and said, "All right, Miss Lady," which meant that dinner was served.

Remembering dinners in Greensboro, I know now (as I didn't know then) how much time and trouble, how much love and care, went into them. Henretta really had too much to do, between the garden and the kitchen, but she was jealous of her prerogatives. Every time Judge tried to hire a yard man to help Henretta, she would drive him off the place. A perfectionist, she trusted no one but herself with a biscuit or a rose. She would be up before dawn, ready to start the day. She would not return to her house in the evening until the last cup had been put away and the dish towel hung up on the back porch to dry. She worked hard to please Miss Lady and Judge but, as with all true artists, the desire for approval motivated her less than her own creative energy.

For Sunday dinner, our first dinner of the summer in Greensboro, Henretta would serve a sumptuous meal with her fresh peach ice cream for dessert. We could never decide what made the ice cream so good—whether there was something about the "taste" of the old hand-turned freezer, whether Georgia peaches were particularly good that year, or whether the cream was especially rich—we only knew that it always rose to state occasions. And if I could somehow manage to be on the back porch just before Henretta announced that dinner was served, she would let me lick the dasher from the freezer and she wouldn't tell on me.

If we did not take second helpings when she passed the serving dishes, an expression of despair, unsuccessfully covered with an even, quivering smile, would come over Henretta's face. Her ego was intimately involved with her creations. She had put her strength, her heart, her life into that peach ice cream, and its rejection was a rejection of herself. She made, I dare say, the best peach ice cream in Georgia.

Miss Lady would say to Henretta, "Just a tiny portion for me. If I have to look at too much food, it just turns my stomach." Then she would down a generous portion, sometimes two.

On one occasion Susan said that just once she wished we could have some store-bought ice cream. Susan loved all the things kids are supposed to love. I didn't. I hated the taste of hot dogs and hamburgers, French's mustard, Heinz ketchup, marshmallows, bubblegum. I was sensitive to the artificial flavors — they seemed to be discordant notes in the harmony I was always listening for.

Susan (and my mother too) thought the food in Greensboro too rich. Confronted with one of Henretta's meals, Susan would say that all she wanted was a grilled cheese sandwich. Miss Lady, who had dined in the great restaurants of France, could not understand how she had produced a granddaughter with such low tastes.

Beside Miss Lady's plate at the dinner table was the brass bell with which she summoned Henretta from the kitchen, tarnished and worn smooth from years of Miss Lady's fingers — she would touch it distractedly, looking around the table to see what needed to be served or who needed to be seen to, then suddenly pick it up and ring decisively with two quick little motions of her wrist. The sound was high and rippling, like a very few notes on a xylophone, but loud enough to be heard in the kitchen and to bring Henretta running.

Susan and I longed to ring the bell, but this was a prerogative belonging exclusively to Miss Lady.

Our cousins, Jimmie and Leila, the children of Aunt Virginia and Uncle Pete, were as fascinated with the little bell as we were. When they came for Sunday dinner, we would sometimes spend the time before dinner was served sitting on the front porch steps imagining the things Henretta would bring to us if we ever got a chance to ring the bell. Jimmie and Leila were a few years younger than Susan and me and were allowed to read comic books and the funny papers, which were forbidden to us by Murlo. Susan and I didn't hesitate to show off the wisdom of our years. Jimmie said that if *he* rang the bell, Henretta would bring in so many bananas that not even Superman could eat them all. Susan said that if *she* rang the bell, Henretta would bring in a plate of sugarplums made by the sugarplum fairies who had been working all morning in the kitchen. "There aren't any fairies in the kitchen," said Jimmie. "Yes, there are," I said. "They're waltzing with the flowers." In a desperate attempt to save her family honor, Leila said that if *she* rang the bell, Henretta would bring in a big bowl of lightning bugs. "What do lightning bugs taste like?" Susan asked. "They taste good," said Leila.

An hour before dinner was to be served, Henretta discovered that the bell was missing. She had looked everywhere, but it was nowhere to be found. Judge called Jimmie, Leila, Susan, and me into the sitting room. Did anyone know where the little bell was? All of us shook our heads solemnly. Miss Lady was in tears. The bell had belonged to her mother, to her mother's mother— Sunday dinner, dinner on any day of the week, could not take place without that bell.

Judge decided that we would all go upstairs to look for the bell. To emphasize the gravity of the occasion, Miss Lady, who never went upstairs, accompanied us. Henretta led the way, followed by Judge and Miss Lady, and then us four children. Henretta searched the linen closets in the hall. In my room she looked under the bed, then cautiously opened my dresser drawers. Judge turned his head away and gazed out the window. Jimmie did the same thing when he realized that this was what a gentleman did in such circumstances.

The procession made its way into Susan's room. Henretta got down on her knees to look under the bed, then in getting up ran her hand over the bedspread. Suddenly, Leila shrieked, "You're getting warm!" We all turned to look at Leila. Her black eyes shone feverishly and there was a red spot on each cheek, like alarm lights. She pranced over to the bed and, smiling beatifically, pulled up the bedspread, reached between the mattress and the box springs, and pulled out the little brass bell. She thrust it into Henretta's hand, then plopped down on the floor. Sitting cross-legged, Leila balanced her face on her hands, and the skirt of her dress puffed out around her like a parachute that had brought her safely down to earth. She gazed studiously out the window, avoiding the eyes of Judge and Miss Lady.

Dinner took place with its accustomed ceremony, and on time. Leila was very quiet and sat up very straight, as if trying to think of something to say appropriate to her starring role. Finally, when Henretta served the peach ice cream, she took a large, dripping bite, brandished her spoon triumphantly, and said, "This stuff tastes like lightning bugs."

Leila was not punished. Judge and Miss Lady forgave a sinner who sinned with so much charm.

Menu II:

The dinner we ate the day Miss Lady's bell disappeared.

⤫

Casserole of Shrimp and Artichokes
with Sherry-Tomato Sauce

Green Beans with Parsley Butter

Henretta's Biscuits

Georgia Pound Cake

Peach Ice Cream

Casserole of Shrimp and Artichokes
with Sherry-Tomato Sauce

*B*ased on a great old recipe in *Four Great Southern Cooks,* this casserole is so flavorful that it needs little accompaniment other than green beans and biscuits.

For the Shrimp Broth:

2 cups white wine

2 cups water

1 large onion, thinly sliced

1 medium carrot, thinly sliced

1 celery stalk, thinly sliced

6 parsley sprigs

1 bay leaf

$\frac{1}{4}$ teaspoon thyme

6 peppercorns

1 tablespoon fresh or dried tarragon

1. Combine all ingredients in a large kettle. Simmer broth for 15 minutes. Then bring to rolling boil, add unpeeled shrimp, and cook about 5 minutes.

2. Allow shrimp to cool in broth. Then peel and devein them.

3 pounds shrimp, cooked in broth, peeled, deveined

4 tablespoons butter

1 clove garlic, minced

4 tablespoons flour

2 cups heavy cream

2 teaspoons Worcestershire sauce
2 teaspoons paprika
¾ teaspoon salt
pinch of cayenne pepper
juice of 2 lemons
1 cup cream sherry
4 tablespoons tomato catsup
1½ pounds artichoke hearts (may use 2 cans)
2 cups sharp Cheddar cheese, grated
1 cup fresh bread crumbs

1. Preheat oven to 350°F.

2. In a medium saucepan melt the butter and add the garlic. Cook for 2–3 minutes, and stir in flour; cook this roux over low heat for 2 minutes, stirring constantly. Stir in the cream, Worcestershire sauce, paprika, salt, cayenne pepper, lemon juice, and sherry. Add the tomato catsup. Stir over low heat for about 5 minutes, until sauce thickens.

3. Butter a large casserole dish. Place a layer of shrimp on the bottom. Cover with a layer of artichoke hearts, then a layer of cheese. Repeat until the dish is filled. Pour the sauce over and sprinkle with bread crumbs. Bake for 30 minutes, or until casserole is hot and bubbling.

8–10 servings

Green Beans with Parsley Butter

*F*resh green beans are best, but you may use frozen whole ones.

> 2 pounds green beans (tender, young ones
>   if possible), washed and trimmed
> 3 tablespoons butter, melted
> 2 tablespoons chopped fresh parsley
> white pepper

1. Fill a large pan with 3 quarts of salted water and bring to boil.
   Add prepared beans. Reduce heat and simmer until tender but
   firm (15–20 minutes). Drain and keep warm.

2. Add chopped parsley and white pepper to melted butter. Pour over
   beans. Serve immediately.

8 servings

Henretta's Biscuits

$\mathcal{H}$enretta always made these look so easy that I never realized their lightness was due to her touch with the dough. Eventually, I mastered them as well. Like the Southern French Bread, they go well with most of the menus in this book.

2 cups flour
1 teaspoon salt
4 teaspoons baking powder
4 tablespoons Crisco shortening
1 cup milk

1. Preheat oven to 425°F.

2. In a large bowl, sift salt and baking powder with flour. Mix in shortening with wooden spoon until well blended.

3. Add just enough milk to make a firm dough. Beat with spoon 12 times. Form into a ball.

4. Put on a lightly floured board, and roll out dough $\frac{1}{4}$-inch thick. With cookie cutter, cut in rounds $1\frac{1}{2}$ inches in diameter.

5. Place in ungreased pan 1 inch apart so biscuit sides will brown. Cook on bottom rack of oven for 5 minutes, then move to middle rack and cook about 10 minutes or until golden brown. Serve hot with butter.

15 biscuits

Georgia Pound Cake

*T*his cake may be frozen and is better if refrigerated before slicing. In fact, it's really better after chilling overnight in the refrigerator. Serve with Peach Ice Cream.

1 box (1 pound) light brown sugar
1 cup white sugar
3 sticks butter
5 large eggs
1 cup milk
3 cups flour
½ teaspoon baking powder
1 teaspoon vanilla
1 cup pecans, chopped

1. Preheat oven to 325°F.

2. In a large bowl, cream butter and both sugars (you may melt the butter). Add eggs one at a time, beating well after each addition. Add milk and flour alternately, beating well. Add baking powder, vanilla, and pecans.

3. Butter two large loaf pans. Pour batter into pans and bake for 1 to 1½ hours, or until toothpick inserted in center comes out clean. Allow to cool before unmolding.

20 servings

Peach Ice Cream

*O*f course, I'm partial to Georgia peaches, but any good, well-ripened Southern peaches will also make a wonderful ice cream.

> 2 pounds ripe peaches
> 2 cups sugar
> 2 quarts heavy cream
> pinch of salt
> 3 teaspoons vanilla extract

1. Peel peaches, remove stones, and mash them. In a large bowl, combine peaches with sugar and mash thoroughly. Add cream, salt, and vanilla, and mix well.

2. Freeze in an ice-cream freezer according to manufacturer's directions.

2 quarts

The Big House, circa 1920

The
Big House

*J*UDGE WAS TALL and slender, with a ruddy complexion and thinning gray hair slicked back with hair oil. He was very stooped, and this, Miss Lady explained, was due to the fact that "Judge always has to bend over to get through doors." When he was sitting down (I can see him in his big green rocker on the front porch), he would lean forward with his elbows on his knees, keeping his head lowered. Judge's jokes and stories had been developed, cultivated, honed over the years. Like an ancient bard he told the same story again and again, but each time it was different. His language fit his physical presence; he never spoke out of character, but he did not give the impression of being self-conscious. He would begin his story softly and unobtrusively, for he knew the power of understatement. The rhythm would gather momentum as he went on. He knew just when to pause, just when to give a hint of the climax. Then suddenly, at the end of his story, as we burst out laughing, he would look up and smile, his eyes blue and bright.

Judge had long conversations with himself on political topics, usually in the bathroom, which was off the sitting room. From almost anywhere downstairs in the house we could hear his voice rise and fall in paroxysms of oratory. One day when Judge had gone off fishing, we heard Henretta in the bathroom opening closets, slamming doors, and banging around with a broom. Miss Lady asked her what she was doing. Henretta said, "I'm trying to find whoever it is Mr. Judge talks to in here."

Judge always fell asleep in church. He could barely get through the hymns, and the preacher would barely be into the sermon before Judge's head dropped down on his chest and he began to snore. His performance was so entertaining that Susan and I didn't really mind sitting through church on a hot Sunday morning. When the time came to take up the collection, Miss Lady would have to lean over, shake Judge's arm, and whisper, "It's time for the collection plate." We never knew whether he would wake up and know where he was or whether he would start out of his sleep and say something like, "Roosevelt is a damn fool." Susan and I would each try, without taking off our white gloves, to work the quarters out of our little crocheted drawstring purses. This accomplished, we would wait in suspense to see if Judge could get himself together in time to take the crisp twenty-dollar bill out of his pocket and have it ready for the collection plate that advanced briskly and inexorably down the aisle.

Although Judge prided himself upon being uneducated, some of his relatives were artists and writers. When Judge's family came to visit we never knew what to expect—whether it was a distant cousin who was a painter and had won the Prix de Rome in 1920, or the photographer niece who lived in London and was a member of the Royal Society.

But Judge was always at pains to show that he was a plain man who didn't like "hifalutin" people. He knew everyone in Greensboro, as had his family before him, and everyone knew him. He called each person by name and he was called by name in return. Every morning he went to the Texaco filling station, a little ways up toward town, and played checkers until dinnertime. I wondered why he had so much free time (I must have been too young to realize he was retired). I asked him how he could afford to play checkers all morning. He laughed and said, "I was smart enough to marry a rich woman." He loved to tease Miss Lady, "You're the one with the money, but I'm the one with the good family."

When I gazed out my bedroom window at Judge's family home, the columned antebellum house across the street, I imagined that at some time in the past my family had been important and distinguished. Judge's ancestors had lived in Georgia since the earliest days. John Evans, who fought in the Revolutionary War, was given a land grant of five hundred acres just south of what is now Atlanta. He established a plantation, married a woman named America Cherry, and had seven children. They lived in log houses before building the main house in 1829. This house was not as grand as some of the later antebellum houses, but it was graceful and comfortable, white clapboard, one story with a high brick foundation, a long, wide central hall and two wings on each side. It was surrounded by boxwood gardens, cotton fields, and forests. When we were taken to visit the family cemetery on the property,

Susan and I were always distressed to see, next to the white Carrara marble tombstones of John Evans and America Cherry and the smaller marble ones of their children, the graves of the slaves marked with small ordinary stones, without names or dates. Miss Lady and Judge did not understand why Susan and I were disturbed by these anonymous graves.

When Judge's branch of the family moved to Greensboro, they built the antebellum house that stood across the street from Miss Lady's. During the Civil War, they lost almost everything and not all of them were able to recoup their fortunes. As Judge's family became more and more impoverished after the war, they clung lovingly to the house and its furnishings, but they could not afford to keep things up. The furniture was upholstered in black horsehair, lumpy and frayed, scratchy and uncomfortable to sit on. The windows, four feet wide and stretching from the floor to the fourteen-foot ceilings, let in the chill in winter and the light and the humid air in summer. A few scraps of damask and Brussels lace still clung to the windows in the two front parlors. The mantelpieces were of Italian marble, but in the east parlor a big brown metal stove with a pipe connected to the fireplace provided the only heat.

A distant relative of Judge's, Cousin Eva, lived alone in that house across the street, which he and Miss Lady maintained for her. She was unmarried with no means of support. Miss Lady's house sparkled and shone with prosperity. Chairs and sofas were reupholstered in elegant fabric, furniture was polished with beeswax, the grand piano was always in tune, and the oriental carpets were cleaned by hand at a special place in Atlanta. But Cousin Eva's house was shabby. I could see an occasional glimmer of its antebellum splendor, like the few bright spots on a tarnished old gilt picture frame, but the house had not really changed since the Civil War.

Judge's mother, Della Asbury, had raised Judge in this house. Miss Della was a large, heavy woman with masses of red hair that she wore in a pouf on top of her head. She died long before I was born, but I knew her from Judge's stories. There were no naps or "spells" of nerves for Miss Della, no trips to Paris, no indolent walks in rose gardens, no witty letters written in delicate script. Miss Della had servants, but she worked right along with them. She was always in her kitchen or her garden. She had been famous for her cooking.

Susan and I played in the basement of the old home. The foundation walls were of brick, two feet thick, the floor of hard beaten clay, and it was always cool there no matter how hot it was outside. A glimmer of light came in through two small windows. In the corners we could barely see Miss Della's old cooking utensils: huge iron cauldrons with their hooks scattered across the floor, griddles and grills, an enormous bowl (for beaten biscuit) carved out of one block of wood, marble slabs, long forks, and copious spoons.

A pianoforte stood in the downstairs hall. Its rectangular shape, with carved legs and smooth, flat surface, fit against the wall opposite the large curving staircase. When I pressed the warped yellow ivory keys they would tinkle, then suddenly hush, then hush completely, giving only this brief, insufficient sound from the past.

I wanted to name the house across the street "the big house," as Tara, Scarlett's home, was called in *Gone With the Wind*. But I was wary of introducing "the big house" into family discourse for fear of being considered pretentious.

Cousin Eva was old and frail and did not do much cooking, and Miss Lady always sent her midday dinner. I asked Miss Lady one day if I could take Cousin Eva her dinner, and she granted me the privilege. Henretta prepared the dinner plate and covered it with a white linen napkin. Then on a smaller plate she put a serving of blackberry-rhubarb cobbler. I put the dinner plate on a tray along with the dessert plate. Balancing the tray, I stepped carefully along the flagstones on the front lawn. I crossed the street, walked through the sanded front yard, up the steps, past the green porch swing and the potted palms, and peeked through the crimson Venetian glass engraved with grape clusters and vines that framed the front door. I turned the handle on the large silver doorbell. After what seemed to be a very long time, I heard Cousin Eva's footsteps coming from the back of the house, and the door opened. She was very slight and stooped, with thin white hair fastened in a small bun at the nape of her neck. Spectacles wobbled on the end of her nose and she leaned toward me, listening through an ear trumpet. She gratefully took the tray from me. Seeing my eyes linger on the dessert plate, she said, "You must eat this yourself. You deserve it for coming such a long way!"

We sat down at the table in the kitchen. Cousin Eva had made lemonade. Her smooth, sweet, tart, heady drink was famous in the family and in Greensboro. While Cousin Eva ate her dinner, I ate the cobbler and drank the lemonade. I was back at Miss Lady's house in time for dinner there. (Of course, I didn't mention the cobbler or the lemonade.)

I knew what I was going to say, but I knew I had to say it at the right time, before Miss Lady became "nervous" about some imagined imperfection at dinner. Perhaps there was a wilted painted daisy in the arrangement in the center of the table, or one of the bread-and-butter plates was placed at the wrong angle to the dinner plate. Maybe the sugar bowl had not been refilled with a perfect mound. And I knew I must speak before Judge dozed off midway through dinner.

Henretta passed the biscuits. The moment seemed propitious.

"I love the big house," I ventured.

"The what?" said Judge.

"The big house. The house across the street."

Although I already knew, I asked Judge when "the big house" was built. He became so interested in relating its history that he neglected to fall asleep. I ate another serving of cobbler for dessert.

For weeks afterward I talked of "the big house." Soon everyone was speaking of "the big house." It was becoming part of family history.

I continued to take Cousin Eva her dinner every day. I continued to eat two desserts—one before dinner, one after. If Cousin Eva suspected what was going on, she never told on me.

Menu III:

Even now, I'd eat the cobbler both before
and after dinner, as I did then.

Pork Chops with Horseradish Mustard,
Dill, and Sour Cream

Stewed Tomatoes

Blackberry-Rhubarb Cobbler

Cousin Eva's Lemonade

Pork Chops with Horseradish Mustard, Dill, and Sour Cream

The chops are braised in sherry, which keeps them tender. The sour cream produces a light and flavorful gravy. This is best served with Henretta's biscuits.

> 6 medium-thick pork chops
> salt
> pepper
> 6 tablespoons horseradish mustard
> 3 tablespoons butter
> 1 cup dry sherry
> 4 tablespoons sour cream
> 3 tablespoons bread crumbs, made from buttered toast
> 2 tablespoons fresh dill, finely chopped

1. Rub pork chops with salt and pepper. Spread them with horseradish mustard, place in large dish, and cover. Refrigerate for 3 to 4 hours.

2. Melt butter in a large enameled casserole. Add chops and brown on both sides. Add sherry, cover, and cook over low heat for 30 minutes. Baste with sour cream and cook for an additional 15 minutes.

3. Transfer chops to heated platter and pour sauce over them. Sprinkle with bread crumbs and dill.

6 servings

Stewed Tomatoes

*T*his recipe comes from a relative of Miss Della's named Monga Ma. I am not sure how they were related or how Monga Ma is related to me, but I do know that she was renowned as a cook.

6 large medium-ripe tomatoes
¼ cup apple cider vinegar
1¼ cups sugar
1 tablespoon bacon grease
½ teaspoon allspice
1 teaspoon salt
¼ teaspoon black pepper

1. Peel and chop tomatoes. Combine with remaining ingredients in a large, heavy skillet and mix well.

2. Cook slowly, uncovered, over low heat, until thick, about 1 hour.

6 servings

Blackberry-Rhubarb Cobbler

There are so many variations on the cobbler, but this is the real one for me—the one I carried to the big house.

1 pound fresh blackberries	*For the Pastry:*
1 pound fresh rhubarb	4 tablespoons butter
1 cup sugar	1 tablespoon cream cheese
	1 cup self-rising flour
	1 egg, beaten
	½ cup milk
	butter to dot
	juice of ½ lemon

1. Preheat oven to 325°F.

2. Wash fruit, and cut the rhubarb into 1-inch pieces. Combine blackberries and rhubarb in a large bowl, mix with the sugar, and let stand while making the pastry.

3. In a medium bowl, cut the 4 tablespoons butter and cream cheese in small bits and cut into the self-rising flour with 2 knives or a pastry cutter. Add egg and mix well, then add milk to make a dough.

4. Press dough with fingers in a thick layer in bottom of a 9-by-12-inch buttered baking dish. Cover pastry with fruit, including juice; dot with bits of butter; sprinkle with lemon juice. (If the fruit has not yielded much juice, you may add ½ cup hot water.)

5. Bake for 45 minutes or until bubbly. Serve warm with boiled custard or cream.

6 servings

Cousin Eva's Lemonade

juice of 5 lemons (about ½ cup juice)
1 cup sugar
4 cups spring water, divided

1. Remove seeds but not pulp from lemon juice.

2. In a medium saucepan, combine sugar with 2 cups water. Bring to boil. Remove from heat and add lemon juice. Cool.

3. Add 2 cups water. Chill. Pour over ice in tall glasses.

8 servings

Luann and Susan

Peaches
and
Cream

*M*ISS ANNIE'S HOUSE, next door to Miss Lady's, was a simple and charming Victorian home, different in style from Miss Lady's but equally graceful. Instead of gables, bay windows, and side porches, a gingerbread-trimmed porch ran all the way across the facade. An aisle of magnificent old cedars covered with ivy led from the street to the front porch. The yard, like Miss Lady's, was filled with cutting gardens and beautiful trees. The two sisters had lived next door to each other from the time they were young women and raised their children together. Their houses, standing well back from the street in the midst of green lawns, were like two young girls in white dresses calling to each other across the garden fence.

In Greensboro it was considered desirable to receive an invitation to Miss Lady's house or to Miss Annie's, and preferably both, for then one could compare. Miss Annie's cook, Grover, was as much a master in the kitchen as Henretta—they were in friendly but intense competition with each other. No one could make biscuits as light as Henretta's, nor cakes so rich and moist, and Grover was famous for his cold buffet.

Miss Annie planned a supper party for a summer evening and asked Miss Lady to bring me to her house the afternoon of the party to "taste" and look at the table. Later in the evening, William, Amy, Susan, and I would be given supper early, and then would be sent upstairs when the guests arrived. We would hang over the bannister, listening to the clinking of china and glass, the laughing and talking voices of grown-up people who seemed to be unbelievably happy. Occasionally we would let a rag doll fall over the railing to the hall floor below, hoping it might conduct to us some of the radiance that pulsed in the dining room and glimmered into the dim hall. But right now, I had the whole party-to-be all to myself.

It was a June day, warm and indolent; this was the season when the sweet Georgia peaches came in. Miss Lady took me by the hand, and we walked over to Miss Annie's house. Grover opened the door and showed us in. I stood on tiptoe, reached up, and hugged him. With her quick step Miss Annie came walking toward us from the back of the house. "Guess what?" she said to me. "Grover has made pecan crescents." Grover said they hadn't turned out as well as he had hoped. "The weather's been so hot, Miss Luann. The dough doesn't handle too good." I knew this to be his requisite show of modesty.

Miss Annie's parlor reminded me of Miss Lady's—velvet and damask upholstery, polished antique tables covered with delicate objets d'art and family photographs, Dutch floral paintings in gilt frames, vases of fresh flowers.

I settled myself in front of the chest that contained Miss Annie's seashell boxes, lined with black velvet. Carefully I ran my hands over the shells, feeling the different textures, each cool to the touch. They were striped and speckled, convoluted and spiked, soft and brilliantly colored. The large abalone shell was wrapped in chamois cloth, its shining mother-of-pearl interior contrasting with its grainy gray outer crust. I held the exquisite conch shell, cream-colored and pink, to my ear, listening to a sound of very distant thunder, like a summer storm still far away. The pent-up shells, all their color and lustre, all their history caught in this velvety parlor, were like the paintings in Miss Lady's art books. This was a leashed world, a world of achieved harmony and surety—the shell's thunder was just the idea of thunder, pleasing because it was under control.

I made my way into the dining room to look at the buffet Grover had laid out on the sideboard. The centerpiece, the galantine of turkey, lay on a long silver platter, covered with cold, thick cream sauce. I wanted to see it sliced, exposing the lovely patterns of the hard-boiled egg yolks, strips of tongue, pistachio nuts, and truffles embedded in the stuffing.

"Can't slice it, Miss Luann," he said. "This turkey has to be sliced just before it's served. You know how the white meat and egg yolks turn brown and stale when the air gets to them."

"Couldn't you cover it?" I asked.

"Nothing that big in this whole house," said Grover.

He looked at the galantine proudly. "I sure am glad you like it."

"It's beautiful," I said softly, awed before his masterpiece.

Grover said, "Now, come to think of it, there is that big old dishpan in the pantry—I could clean it up real good—"

"You mean, cover the turkey with the dishpan?"

"Exactly," said Grover. "Then we could slice it up right now and see that specialty."

"But Miss Annie—"

"Miss Annie won't know," said Grover.

"But if Miss Annie sees the dishpan in the dining room, in the middle of the sideboard—"

"Miss Annie never comes into the dining room until the last minute, just as the doorbell rings for the first time. By then that dishpan will be long gone."

Grover wanted the galantine to be the finest he had ever made, and each serving to be pristine, freshly sliced. But he wanted even more to show me his artistry, to prove what I already knew, that he was a master chef. I knew that Grover would have his cake and eat it, too.

He went into the kitchen and banged around in the pantry until he found the huge, rusty, old enamel dishpan, then scrubbed it with steel wool and wiped it dry. He brought it into the dining room and propped it gingerly against a leg of the sideboard while he cut into the galantine. The almost-round slices lay against each other in a long row, green, yellow, rose, and black studding the pale pink stuffing, surrounded by the white turkey breast meat, the whole lying in the bed of cream sauce.

I said, "It's like one of those dishes Judge and Miss Lady order when they go to a restaurant in Paris."

"I believe that is correct, Miss Luann," said Grover, trying to contain with seemly modesty his bursting pride. He garnished the platter with a few sprigs of parsley and reluctantly covered the galantine, fitting the dishpan upside-down over the silver tray.

I went into the parlor to join Miss Lady and Miss Annie. Grover followed in a few moments, pushing a tea cart. He gave me a bowl of fresh peaches, sliced and sugared, and a silver spoon. His white-gloved hands made barely a sound as he handed the dishes round. He set a plate of pecan cookies on the heart-shaped tea table.

I looked down into the bowl of beautiful tree-ripened peaches. Each slice was bright yellow, edged with red, lapped with pale pink juice. Cutting with my spoon, I suddenly saw a long green worm working its way out of one of the slices. I almost lost my head. I almost dropped the bowl. But I knew that I must not be rude, that I must not let Miss Annie or Grover think that anything about their house, their hospitality, their peaches displeased me.

"Cream, Miss Luann?" Grover stood in front of me, the large pitcher poised. Trembling, I raised my bowl. Grover poured in a little cream. I raised my bowl higher. Grover chuckled.

"Miss Luann loves cream."

The thick cream flowed down, completely submerging the peaches, the spoon, the worm.

I lowered my head over the bowl, my face burning. Grover moved away. Miss Lady and Miss Annie chatted brightly, confident that there had never been a snake in the Garden of Eden. Quietly I covered the bowl with my napkin and set it down on the tea table.

Grover picked up the plate of pecan crescents and offered it to me, disappointed I hadn't already helped myself. I knew that not only must I take one, I must eat one.

I had no appetite. I didn't think I could swallow. But the first bite was good, the second better. Grover watched the expression on my face. He seemed satisfied that the pecan crescents were as good as they had ever been— his talents were not slipping, his touch with pastry was still fresh and fine.

My nausea was gone. I had done the right thing. I was cool and innocent and proud.

Menu IV:

A Summer Buffet:
What we ate the day Grover sliced the galantine just for me.

Galantine of Turkey with Chaudfroid Sauce
Tomatoes with Caviar
Chilled Sweetbreads Salad
Peaches with Sabayon Sauce
Hot Raspberry Soufflé with Cold Raspberry Sauce
Pecan Crescents

A Fall Buffet:
Once when Aunt Virginia came to visit
from Jonesboro, she prepared this sumptuous menu for us.

Aunt Virginia's Terrine of Pheasant
Caviar Tart
Cousin Mildred's Chicken Salad
Tomato Aspic
Watermelon Rind Pickle
Cousin Wilma's Sugar Plum Cake
Chestnut Cream

A Summer Buffet

Galantine of Turkey with Chaudfroid Sauce

The centerpiece of a cold buffet. Sadly, few people serve such complicatedly elegant dishes these days. Serve with Leslie's Southern French Bread.

1 12-pound turkey, boned
1 pound veal, finely ground
½ pound cooked ham, finely ground
salt
pepper
3 yolks of hard-boiled eggs
4 or 5 truffles (may use canned)
a handful of shelled pistachio nuts
4 strips of cooked tongue
watercress or sprigs of fresh parsley

For the Turkey Stock:

carcass and bones of boned turkey
8 cups water
2 stalks celery, chopped, with tender leaves
1 large onion, sliced
1 large carrot, chopped
4 peppercorns
1 bay leaf
3 sprigs fresh parsley
½ teaspoon thyme
1 clove garlic, peeled

For the Chaudfroid Sauce:

1½ cups turkey stock
1 cup heavy cream
1 small onion, diced
¼ cup carrots, diced
¼ teaspoon dried thyme or 2 sprigs fresh
 thyme or tarragon
salt
pepper
1 envelope gelatin
¼ cup dry white wine or white vermouth

1. Have the butcher bone the turkey entirely, leaving the skin in place, cutting it open down the center of the back. A good butcher can do this. If necessary, use boned breast only.

2. Reserve the bones for well-flavored turkey stock. To make stock, put all ingredients in a large pot. Bring to boil, reduce heat, partially cover, and simmer for 1½ hours. Strain.

3. In a large bowl, mix the finely ground veal and ham; season well with salt and pepper.

4. Wet a board and spread the turkey open on it; sprinkle with salt and pepper. Spread the veal and ham mixture over it; arrange the 3 egg yolks in the middle; put the truffles, pistachio nuts, and strips of tongue along the sides. Roll up, lapping the back over the breast, wrap in buttered cheesecloth, and secure with string.

5. Bring the turkey stock to a boil in a large pot. Add the turkey, reduce heat, and simmer for 1½ hours. Remove turkey, reserving stock, and roll in a clean cloth; press a little until cold. Remove cheesecloth. Remove skin from turkey. Chill.

6. Serve on a large platter, cover with Chaudfroid Sauce, and garnish if you wish with additional truffles and watercress or sprigs of parsley. Slice into ½-inch slices.

7. To make Chaudfroid Sauce, place the first 5 ingredients in a medium saucepan and bring to boiling point. Reduce heat and simmer until liquid has reduced to 2 cups, about 15 minutes. Add salt and pepper to taste.

8. In a small bowl, soften gelatin in wine and add to the sauce. Heat thoroughly; strain and chill.

12 servings (approximately 2 cups of sauce)

Tomatoes with Caviar

Of course, homegrown tomatoes are essential in this dish.

> 4 large, ripe tomatoes, peeled
> 3 hard-boiled eggs
> 12 lettuce leaves (Boston lettuce)
> salt
> mayonnaise (homemade, see page 83,
>   Chilled Sweetbreads Salad)
> 3–4 ounces black caviar

1. Slice tomatoes thickly to make approximately 3 slices to each tomato.

2. Rice hard-boiled eggs.

3. Arrange tender lettuce leaves on a platter, lay a slice of tomato on each leaf, and lightly salt each tomato. Cover top of each slice with riced egg. Put a spoonful of mayonnaise in the center. Top with a spoonful of caviar.

12 servings

Chilled Sweetbreads Salad

Don't be afraid of sweetbreads. They are delicious when given this special treatment.

                2 pounds sweetbreads
                2 tablespoons white wine vinegar
                1 cup Vinaigrette Dressing with fresh herbs
                   (see recipe below)
                2 cups mayonnaise (homemade, see recipe below)
                1 cup heavy cream, whipped
                2 cucumbers, peeled, seeded, diced, drained
                4 hard-boiled eggs, chopped
                2 small onions, grated
                2 celery hearts, diced
                juice of 2 lemons
                1 cup slivered almonds
                salt
                cayenne pepper

1. In a medium bowl, soak sweetbreads for half an hour in cold water to which the vinegar has been added.

2. Bring 4 cups of salted water to a boil and add sweetbreads. Reduce heat and simmer for 20 minutes.

3. Remove from heat and plunge sweetbreads into cold water. Drain and remove outer membrane. Break into small pieces.

4. Marinate in Vinaigrette Dressing for 1 hour or longer.

5. Drain the sweetbreads and combine with mayonnaise, whipped cream, cucumbers, eggs, onions, celery hearts, lemon juice, and almonds. Season well with salt and cayenne pepper. Serve on a large platter garnished with lettuce leaves.

10 servings

For the Vinaigrette Dressing (1 cup):

¼ cup white wine vinegar
¾ cup oil (light olive oil, peanut oil, or canola oil)
salt
pepper
finely chopped fresh herbs: dill, tarragon, parsley,
    marjoram, etc.

1. Dissolve salt and pepper in vinegar.
2. With wire whisk, beat oil in a thin stream into vinegar.
3. Add herbs.

For the Mayonnaise (2 cups):

4 egg yolks
2 cups oil (light olive oil, peanut oil, or canola oil)
salt
pepper
2 tablespoons (or more) white wine vinegar

1. Use an electric mixer. In a small bowl, beat egg yolks on low speed for 2 minutes.
2. Add oil by droplets, beating all the time.
3. Season to taste with salt, pepper, and white wine vinegar.

Peaches with Sabayon Sauce

*A*n excellent light dessert.

> 6 egg yolks
> 1 cup sugar
> pinch of salt
> 1 cup cream sherry (Bristol Cream, if possible)
> 4 large ripe peaches
> 1 cup heavy cream, whipped, unsweetened

1. In the top of a double boiler, beat the egg yolks until thick. Slowly beat in the sugar, pinch of salt, and cream sherry. Cook over simmering water until thick (160°F on a candy thermometer), stirring all the time. Chill.

2. Dip peaches for a few seconds in boiling water, and carefully remove skins. Halve the peaches and remove the stones. Arrange halves on a platter, cover with the chilled Sabayon Sauce, then with the unsweetened whipped cream.

8 servings

Hot Raspberry Soufflé with Cold Raspberry Sauce

*T*he contrast of the hot soufflé with the cold sauce makes this dessert unusual.

> 1 pound raspberries, fresh or frozen, unsweetened
> $\frac{1}{2}$ cup confectioners' sugar
> 4 egg yolks
> $\frac{1}{3}$ cup granulated sugar
> 5 egg whites
> pinch of salt
> 1 tablespoon unsalted butter
> extra confectioners' sugar

1. Puree raspberries in a food processor or blender and strain to remove seeds. Add confectioners' sugar and blend well. Set aside ½ cup of the puree for the soufflé; the rest is for the sauce.
2. Preheat oven to 400°F.
3. Place egg yolks, granulated sugar, and the ½ cup raspberry puree in a medium-sized heavy saucepan. Beat mixture for about 3 minutes. Heat about 10 minutes, over very low heat, beating all the time, until mixture reaches the consistency of mayonnaise. (Do not let it get too hot.) Remove from heat.
4. In a medium bowl, beat egg whites with pinch of salt until stiff. Gently fold egg whites into raspberry mixture.
5. Butter a soufflé dish with the unsalted butter and dust it with confectioners' sugar. Pour in soufflé. The dish should be at least three-quarters full. Bake in preheated oven for 20 minutes. Remove from oven and sprinkle lightly with confectioners' sugar. Serve immediately with sauce.

6 servings

For the Sauce (make ahead):
1 cup raspberry puree
1 cup red currant jelly
1½ teaspoons cornstarch
orange liqueur
lemon juice

1. In a medium saucepan, combine raspberry puree with currant jelly. Bring to a boil.
2. In a small bowl, blend cornstarch with a little cold water to make a paste. Stir into sauce and simmer until thick and clear. Add orange liqueur to taste and a few drops of lemon juice. Chill.
3. Serve cold with soufflé.

Pecan Crescents

A Southern version of Mexican Wedding Cookies, these are so light that they seem to miraculously dissolve in your mouth.

> 2 sticks butter
> 5 heaping tablespoons confectioners' sugar
> 2 cups flour
> 1 cup pecans, finely chopped
> 1½ teaspoons vanilla
> extra confectioners' sugar

1. In a medium bowl, cream butter and sugar. Add flour, mixing well. Add pecans and vanilla. Cover and chill the dough for half an hour.

2. Preheat oven to 325°F.

3. Roll a small amount of dough between palms and form into a crescent. Repeat to make about two dozen.

4. Place on baking sheets and bake until slightly brown, about 10–15 minutes.

5. When cool, roll in confectioners' sugar.

About 2 dozen cookies

A Fall Buffet

Aunt Virginia's Terrine of Pheasant

This magnificent terrine is appropriate for a festive occasion and is worth the effort. I believe Aunt Virginia said the recipe came from Antoine's Restaurant in New Orleans.

> 3 small fresh truffles, or 1 large truffle
> 2 tablespoons unsalted butter
> 2 pounds raw veal, ground
> 3 pounds raw pork, ground
> 2 pounds raw pheasant meat, ground
> 2 eggs
> 1 tablespoon salt
> 1 tablespoon black pepper
> 1 cup cognac
> 2 cups pecans, coarsely chopped, parboiled in
>   salted water and drained
> 2 pounds bacon, thinly sliced
> 3 thick slices cooked ham, cut in strips
> 3 slices raw pheasant breast, cut in strips

1. Peel and chop truffles coarsely. Cook in unsalted butter 2 to 3 minutes; add a little cognac and cook 1 minute longer.

2. Preheat oven to 350°F.

3. In a large bowl, combine all ingredients except the last three until well blended. The mixture should have the consistency of a meatloaf.

4. Line a very large terrine, 12 inches in diameter (or three or four small ones), with bacon slices, then cover with 1 inch of stuffing mixture. Lay strips of ham, bacon, and pheasant breast, $\frac{1}{2}$ inch apart, on the stuffing. Alternate layers of stuffing and strips, finishing with a 1-inch layer of stuffing. Cover the top with slices of bacon.

5. Place terrine in a shallow pan filled with boiling water and bake about 2 hours, or until fat rises to top and meat shrinks away from sides.

6. Let cool for several hours, then refrigerate for 12 hours. Remove some of the fat before serving. Serve from terrine.

20 servings

Caviar Tart

*A*n elegant tart which may also be served as an hors d'oeuvre or with cocktails or champagne.

> 6 hard-boiled eggs, riced
> 1 pound black caviar
> juice of ½ lemon
> 1 cup sour cream, at room temperature
> paprika
> fresh minced dill
> 1 lemon, sliced thin, seeded, and each slice halved

1. Butter a 9-inch Pyrex pie plate and firmly press the riced hard-boiled eggs onto the bottom and sides of the plate to form a "crust." Cover and refrigerate for 24 hours.

2. The next day, carefully mix the caviar with the lemon juice and spread evenly over the crust. Spoon sour cream evenly over the caviar. Cover and refrigerate for at least 1 hour.

3. Before serving, sprinkle the top with a little paprika and decorate the edges of the pie with finely minced dill.

4. Arrange lemon slices around the edge of tart.

5. Cut into small wedges and serve with toast or crackers.

12 servings

Cousin Mildred's Chicken Salad

*M*y cousin Mildred served this on grand occasions in Atlanta.

> 6 whole chicken breasts, poached in broth, skinned,
>   boned, chopped
> 3 celery hearts, finely chopped
> 4 hard-boiled eggs, chopped
> 1 cup peeled slivered almonds or chopped salted pecans
> 1 cup mayonnaise (homemade, see page 83,
>   Chilled Sweetbreads Salad)

1. Mix first four ingredients, add Cooked Dressing (see recipe below),
   and let stand in refrigerator overnight.

2. When ready to serve, add 1 cup mayonnaise. Serve chilled in a glass bowl or
   on a large platter garnished with lettuce leaves and parsley or fresh tarragon.

15 servings

For the Cooked Dressing:

> 9 egg yolks or 4 whole eggs
> 6 tablespoons sugar
> 1 tablespoon cornstarch
> 3 teaspoons salt
> 3 teaspoons dry mustard
> 1 teaspoon celery seed
> $\frac{1}{2}$ teaspoon white pepper
> 1 cup milk
> 5 tablespoons butter
> 1 cup white wine vinegar

1. In a large bowl, beat eggs well.

2. In a medium bowl, mix dry ingredients. Beat dry ingredients into eggs, then add milk slowly, using an electric mixer.

3. Transfer mixture to double-boiler and cook over medium heat, stirring constantly, adding the butter in small bits until mixture is thick and measures 160°F on a candy thermometer. (This is like making a hollandaise; be sure to use a candy thermometer.) Take dressing off heat.

4. In a small saucepan, heat vinegar *very* slowly over low heat; when warm, add vinegar a little at a time to dressing, stirring to blend.

5. Put cold water in bottom of the double-boiler. Cook the dressing again slowly in top of double-boiler over medium heat, stirring occasionally until it thickens (120°F on a candy thermometer). Allow it to cool before mixing with chicken and other ingredients.

Tomato Aspic

A real aspic made with fresh vegetables, not the sweet lemon Jell-O variety.

> 4 large ripe tomatoes, peeled, seeded, chopped
> (retain all juice)
> 2 stalks celery, chopped
> 1 small green pepper, chopped
> 2 tablespoons grated onion
> 2 tablespoons red wine vinegar
> salt
> cayenne pepper
> ½ cup water
> 2 envelopes gelatin
> 2 teaspoons chopped fresh basil
> 1 cup mayonnaise (homemade, see p. 83, Chilled
> Sweetbreads Salad) with 2 tablespoons capers

1. In a large bowl, combine chopped celery and green peppers with tomatoes and juice. Add onion, vinegar, salt, and cayenne pepper. Puree in a blender or food processor.

2. Pour the water in a small saucepan and add gelatin. Stir over low heat until gelatin dissolves. Stir into the tomato mixture. Add basil.

3. Rinse out a 10-inch mold with cold water and shake out excess. Pour tomato mixture into mold and refrigerate until aspic is set.

4. Unmold aspic onto a platter, surround with lettuce leaves, and serve with caper mayonnaise.

8 servings

Watermelon Rind Pickle

There are many recipes for watermelon rind pickle, but this is absolutely the best, very dark and rich. It was given to me by the same friend who gave me the recipe for Green Tomato Chutney. She is a tiny, delicate lady, but she can do big things in the kitchen.

1 large green striped watermelon with a thick rind	*For the Syrup (for 1 gallon of rind):*
1 cup pickling lime (available at grocer)	5 cups apple cider vinegar
	1 tablespoon whole cloves
	2 sticks cinnamon
1 tablespoon alum (available at pharmacy)	10 cups sugar
	1 tablespoon whole allspice
1 tablespoon powdered ginger	2½ cups water

1. Peel the melon and cut the rind in 1-inch squares.
2. Put rind in a large bowl. Cover with water and add pickling lime. Soak rind for 12 hours.
3. Put rind and lime water in a large enamel kettle and bring almost to boil. Drain. Wash thoroughly.
4. Add alum to 1 gallon water in kettle. Bring to boil, add rind, and scald for 5 minutes, cooking at 185° or just below boiling. Drain rind and wash thoroughly.
5. Add powdered ginger to 1 gallon of water. Put in kettle and bring to boil. Add rind, reduce heat, and simmer for 30 minutes.
6. Cool rind thoroughly by plunging it in cold water 7 times (may use ice).
7. After this preparation, cook rind in syrup. Tie cloves and allspice in cheesecloth. Put all ingredients for syrup in kettle, bring to boil, add rind, reduce heat, and simmer for about 3 hours. Remove spices after 2 hours.
8. Pack rind into sterilized jars and cover with syrup. Seal jars.

8–10 pints

Cousin Wilma's Sugar Plum Cake

Cousin Wilma always sends this cake at Christmas. It is so moist that it keeps well covered in the refrigerator.

2 cups sugar

2 sticks unsalted butter, softened

3 large eggs

2 cups flour

2 teaspoons cinnamon

2 teaspoons nutmeg

2 teaspoons ground cloves

1 teaspoon soda

½ teaspoon salt

1 cup buttermilk or yogurt

1 cup chopped pecans

1 cup cooked, chopped prunes

For the Icing:

1 stick unsalted butter

1 cup sugar

½ cup buttermilk or yogurt

½ teaspoon soda

1. Preheat oven to 325°F.

2. In a large bowl, mix together sugar, butter, and eggs.

3. In a medium bowl, sift together flour, cinnamon, nutmeg, cloves, soda, and salt.

4. Add flour mixture to sugar mixture alternately with buttermilk or yogurt. Add pecans and prunes.

5. Pour in a buttered 10-inch tube pan and bake for 1 hour, or until toothpick inserted in center comes out clean. Leave cake in pan and punch holes in the top with a skewer so icing can penetrate.

6. To make the icing, put all ingredients in a medium saucepan and bring to a boil. Cool slightly. Pour icing over warm cake.

7. Cool thoroughly before unmolding. This cake freezes well.

15 servings

Chestnut Cream

Chestnuts, so valued by French cooks, were served often in the old South. Both pureed and preserved, they are available at specialty stores.

2 envelopes gelatin
¼ cup cold water
¼ cup boiling water
5 egg yolks
1 cup sugar
pinch of salt
½ cup bourbon whiskey
3 cups heavy cream, whipped
1 cup preserved chestnuts (drained if in syrup), cut fine
crystallized violets

1. In a small bowl, soften gelatin in cold water. Add boiling water.

2. In a large bowl, beat the egg yolks until thick and lemon-colored; slowly beat in the sugar and the pinch of salt, and continue beating until mixture is thick and pale yellow. Beat in the whiskey very slowly (this cooks the egg yolks). Add dissolved gelatin.

3. Fold the cut-up chestnuts and the whipped cream delicately into the egg mixture with a spatula.

4. Rinse out a 10-inch ring mold with cold water and shake out excess. Pour in Chestnut Cream, cover, and allow to congeal in refrigerator for several hours.

5. To serve, unmold onto a serving platter. Garnish with crystallized violets.

8 servings

My mother, Luann Foster, and my father,
Edward Evans, Guam, World War II

Two
Grandmothers

$\mathcal{T}$HERE IS NO doubt that Murlo was jealous of the ease and security of Miss Lady's life. Miss Lady was the adored child of parents who had married for love. Her father's business was successful in the 1880s as the South was recovering from the Civil War, so Miss Lady's family did not know the humiliating poverty that disheartened and limited the prospects of many Southern families. Miss Lady, born in 1887, grew up in a lovely old Georgia town. She was surrounded by beautiful houses and gardens, elegant clothes, good food, loving relatives and friends. Even the death of her mother when she was seventeen was softened by the strength of her father's presence. Papa had been both father and mother to her, giving her educational advantages, taking her on lovely trips both here and abroad.

Murlo's youth was much more difficult. The oldest of twelve children, she was her father's favorite, but she also carried the heaviest family responsibilities. When she was twelve, as we had heard many times, she began to manage her father's house and land on the White River in Izard County north of Little Rock, Arkansas. Her mother was too easygoing and too often pregnant. Murlo was responsible for the health and well-being of a large number of people. During the typhoid epidemics (her father had unwittingly dug the well on ground that was lower than the stables and the barn), the house was converted to a hospital; pallets were laid down in all the rooms and wet sheets hung at the windows against the heat. Servants and tenant farmers lay beside the ladies and gentlemen of the house. Those who did not die got up as soon as they showed signs of recovery and began nursing the ones who were still sick. Murlo's favorite younger brother, Jimmy, died of typhoid when he was twelve. I have visited his tombstone, in an abandoned cemetery near a little white frame country church, which reads, "I am going home, to die no more." I think often of that small, weathered tombstone. And I think of the dark circles around Murlo's deep-set, dark eyes and of the trouble those eyes had looked upon.

MISS LADY LIVED a sheltered girlhood in Greensboro. It's perhaps an indication of Miss Lady's sense of the preciousness of her own life that she wrote an autobiography. *This Is My Story* describes her charmed childhood and the town she knew as a child and young woman:

One of my happiest memories is waiting for the lamplighter to come around to the lamppost nearest our house. . . . The old colored man had a ladder which he would lean against the post to light the lamp, and on a snowy evening it was a picturesque sight. . . . Mr. Joplin had a market next to Papa's Bank (later made into a National Bank). . . . Mr. Joplin had a colored man who would come around every morning with an order book and Mama would write down her order for the day. Mr. Joplin was quite a character. He seemed fond of me as a child and called me "Mary, Mildred, Rachel, Ann, Colia, Elizabeth, Frotas, Frances Copeland." This of course pleased and amused me.

There were several stores in Greensboro that were very interesting. . . . Rossman's was a fine store for a small town. They carried what we called "French Candy." You would select the kinds you wanted and they would box it for you. They had fruits of all kinds and beautiful glass-ware, china and ornaments for the home. The pair of milk glass dishes (blue and pink) with scalloped edges came from there and were Mama's. Once every Christmas Mama and Papa would take us up to Rossman's to see the Christmas things. . . .

A memorable day was when we had the first Coca-Cola, at Rice's Drug Store. Mrs. Vince Hall, a neighbor of ours, used to send a pitcher up for it every morning. It was long after this that you could get it in bottles. . . .

Our old Church was a brick building with green blinds and tall steeple that stood on the lot where the Dowdys now live. A beautiful church, similar to the Presbyterian Church here. It holds many memories for me. It had a slave gallery and I well remember when it was customary for the men to sit on one side and the women on the other. . . . Sister and Mr. Merritt were married there December 31, 1902. Sister had a beautiful wedding with reception afterwards at home. There was a full moon that night and snow on the ground. As it was such a short distance, Mama had mill cloth put down from our house to the Church. . . .

Papa had a pair of bay horses, and we had a carriage and surrey. Uncle Claiborne was the colored man who looked after the horses, and he could usually be found in the carriage house polishing the harness. Emma Peek was our cook. She lived in a house on the corner of the vacant lot across the street by the cedar tree, that is still there. . . . Every Thursday afternoon Emma took all the cooking utensils out in the yard and scrubbed them perfectly clean.

When Miss Lady spoke of a man and woman marrying, she always said, "They fell in love and got married." Murlo would have considered such talk sentimental. After she graduated from college, Murlo decided not to marry. Instead, she chose to have a career as a teacher at a school for the blind in Little Rock, where she worked for several years. I don't know what finally changed her mind about marriage; perhaps the fact that Mr. Foster (as she called her husband) was a wealthy man. She had turned down one offer from a man she thought would never amount to anything. As fate would have it, he married one of Murlo's sisters and became a successful real estate developer in California. Perhaps Mr. Foster seemed more acceptable—a banker who came from an aristocratic New England family and was well educated (Murlo would settle for nothing less than money, aristocracy, *and* culture). And for several years he gave her the life a "highborn" person (her term) expected and deserved. But by the time my mother was born, Mr. Foster had lost his money;

he was a kind man who lent generously to "friends" who never repaid him. The family moved to a Kansas farm, where Murlo was trapped once again in a hard life. Murlo did not forgive him.

She said (often in front of her children) that if she had had her way she would never have had children, and she would have been happy as a teacher. However, once Murlo was into difficulty, she concentrated all her strength and intelligence on her situation. When I heard my mother tell stories about her parents, I sensed that there was no romantic love between them but that they were totally dedicated to the idea of establishing a family and bringing up the children. After the move to Kansas, Murlo put her life force into maintaining high standards on a low income.

Murlo was not warm or affectionate or fun. She was committed. If a member of her extended family became ill, she would travel by Pullman across the country to nurse the patient, who usually recovered because the nursing care was excellent, not because Murlo's presence had infused them with a rejuvenating love of life.

As the years passed, Murlo became proud of her poverty and relished her martyrdom. Soft, pleasure-loving Miss Lady was rich, selfish, and indolent, whereas she, Murlo, was poor, selfless, and hardworking.

DURING THE WORLD WAR II years when my father was in the South Pacific with the Third Marines, we visited a lot in Greensboro, usually with Murlo. In the spring of 1946, my Aunt Virginia was very pregnant with her second baby—"'bout ready to birth," Henretta said. Miss Lady's cotton mill (or nearly hers—she was the major stockholder) was going to be sold to an Eastern conglomerate, and two of the executives from New York were in Greensboro to close the deal. Miss Lady was to have them to supper on a Friday evening. Her company meals were works of art, and she did not hesitate to sacrifice the comfort of the people around her to achieve her masterpiece.

The main body of the dinner was Henretta's, and both Henretta and Miss Lady would have had it no other way. The table setting and the buttermilk pie were Virginia's assignments. The dessert, a Southern specialty, was to be served for the edification of the New Yorkers. As usual, Miss Lady assigned herself no job other than to delegate tasks.

On the afternoon of the big dinner, Murlo and Virginia met in the downstairs hall near Miss Lady's bedroom. Murlo had been upstairs most of the day making dresses for Susan and me on Virginia's sewing machine. Virginia's pregnancy was near its term, and she was very uncomfortable. She held her hands at the small of her back to relieve the strain. Her cheeks were wet with tears.

"What's the matter, honey?" Murlo asked.

"Nothing," Virginia said. "I'm going up and stretch out for a while. I've done the centerpiece and set the table. I'll have the buttermilk pie made in plenty of time."

Angrily, Murlo raised her voice, loud enough for Miss Lady to hear in her bedroom, "I can't imagine why you are expected to do such strenuous work in your condition. Go to bed and get a good rest. I'll make the pie."

Murlo went to work in the kitchen. All the while, small sounds of distress emanated from Miss Lady's room. Before long, Susan and I came in from the yard and passed Miss Lady's bedroom, the door now closed, the small sounds still audible. Susan cracked the door and peeked in. She closed the door and shrugged. "She's having a good cry."

Dinner was a great success. Ironclad good manners masked the grandmothers' feelings. But it was clear to anyone who knew them and observed them closely that Murlo was high on her horse of righteous indignation and Miss Lady was nursing her hurt feelings.

The gentlemen from New York were nevertheless impressed. Even if they were not the sort of Northerners who thought that people in the South live in log cabins and don't wear shoes, they were certainly surprised to encounter such cuisine in a small Georgia town. The country ham was sliced paper thin, and the beaten biscuits had turned out perfectly. The stewed corn was a delicacy they could not have anticipated, given its pedestrian name.

All through the supper, Murlo maintained the noble countenance of a woman who would *never* sacrifice her own daughter's health for the preparation of a meal intended to impress out-of-town guests, guests who were not even close friends of the family. She served the buttermilk pie and received the enthusiastic compliments graciously, with just a touch of humility.

She turned to Miss Lady. "Will you have another piece of buttermilk pie, Mrs. Evans?"

"No thank you, Mrs. Foster," Miss Lady replied meekly. "I've had all the buttermilk pie I can enjoy."

Triumphantly, Murlo turned to the New York guests, who asked for second helpings.

A week later, on Easter Sunday, Aunt Virginia's little girl was born. In the happy atmosphere that attends the safe arrival of a baby, Murlo and Miss

Lady were chatting like old friends in front of the fire in Miss Lady's bedroom.

"I thank the Lord they're both fine," Miss Lady said. "And how wonderful that her birthday will always be on Easter."

"Oh, but it won't," Murlo said, "Easter is a moveable feast," pointing out, oh so subtly, Miss Lady's ignorance of the church calendar.

THEIR LAST CONFRONTATION, as I heard about it, is almost too sad to tell—a gloves-off clash over the ladies' adoration of their sons. The times were out of joint. World War II was over, the men were home, and their families were encountering problems they had never anticipated. The treatments for minds damaged in combat were not yet developed. My father, like so many other soldiers, came back from the Pacific in excellent physical condition and a nervous wreck. He drank more and more as he struggled to adjust to civilian life. While my parents were trying to cope with their problems, Murlo took Susan and me to stay in Greensboro until things got better. Murlo was grim and worried. But she was also worried about her own son, my Uncle Mike, who was becoming an alcoholic himself.

Uncle Mike was a novelist, and quite successful in the '30s and '40s, but he thought he was a better writer than he really was. He had a gift for rich Southern language (rather like Thomas Wolfe), but sentimentality and intellectual flabbiness prevented him from becoming a writer of the first rank. Murlo, with her astute mind, probably realized this, but she would not admit it.

At this time, Miss Lady was beginning to suspect, without daring to put her suspicions into words, that her son's experience in the marines had ruined him. Like his mother, my father was a sensitive man, accustomed to physical comfort, courtesy, and subtlety of nuance in human relationships. Miss Lady said, "Edward was so tenderly raised. He couldn't take the rough stuff." He probably would have done well at a desk job during the war, but wrongheaded ideas about masculinity and service to his country led him to enlist in the marines. He tried to prove himself by doing things he was not fit to do. World War II's effect on my father frightened Miss Lady: her world, the world she had prepared her son to live in, seemed insecure. For the first time, her gentle, graceful life was threatened by brutal reality.

On the occasion of their last meeting, when Murlo and Miss Lady sat down to talk in Greensboro, Miss Lady began to cry. She said she felt so sorry for my poor father in the grip of this affliction. Murlo responded that if *she* were the emotional type, she would be crying for his wife and children. She truly believed, she added, that my father could pull himself together for his family's sake.

He didn't seem able to do that, Miss Lady replied. Surely Murlo would understand, her own son having the same problem.

Murlo stood up. "How dare you compare my son with yours!" she cried.

My father died the following year. Uncle Mike lived on for several more years, in a kind of living death of alcoholism and egotism. These disasters should have brought the two women together. Murlo should have said, "For God's sake, let us sit upon the ground / And tell sad stories of the death of sons." Miss Lady should have said, "Would God I had died for thee, O Absalom, my son."

But, of course, they did not say such things. Murlo's energy and Miss Lady's grace were reduced to bitterness and stony silence.

It was in raising their grandchildren that they came back to life, Murlo in Nashville, Miss Lady in Greensboro. Murlo read to me long passages from the King James version of the Bible, hoping this language would train my ear, hoping the family would produce a real writer. On long, hot summer afternoons, Miss Lady told Susan and me her story; she showed us her scrapbooks in which she had pasted pictures of the great paintings she had seen and of the castles and cathedrals she had visited. She spoke of her antiques and her family history, hoping we would learn to appreciate the inheritance our father never came into.

Although enmity usually prevailed between Murlo and Miss Lady, occasionally their guilt, or a sudden awareness of their foolishness, would overcome them and they would make an effort at reconciliation or at least attempt a pleasant interlude. But the old Adam (or what Judge called "the old Eve") would nearly always triumph and they would return to their fallen world of competition and jealousy.

As long as I knew her, Murlo slept only three or four hours a night. As a guest in Greensboro, she was entitled to breakfast in bed, but she would have none of that self-indulgence. She would be up at six to join Henretta in the kitchen, where she made her own breakfast. She thought that Miss Lady worked Henretta far too hard, and that with the callousness typical of a selfish person, Miss Lady sacrificed Henretta's welfare to achieve her perfectly run luxurious household.

Miss Lady slept long and well. She would awake at eight and linger for an hour over breakfast in bed. Then, after a leisurely bath, she would dress and be ready to start the day around ten. One morning—it must have been between ten-thirty and eleven—Miss Lady met Murlo in the downstairs hall. Hoping once again to start a pleasant conversation with Murlo, she said brightly, "When did you get up?"

Murlo replied, "I've been up for seventy years."

Menu V:

The supper that impressed the Northerners.

❧

Grapefruit Salad with Roquefort Dressing

Country Ham

Beaten Biscuits

Green Tomato Chutney

Henretta's Stewed Corn

Baby Lima Beans

My Mother's Yellow Squash Casserole

Buttermilk Pie

Grapefruit Salad with Roquefort Dressing

*T*his is a secret recipe given to Murlo by a friend. I hope she'll forgive me for sharing it after all these years.

2 heads Boston lettuce
3 pink grapefruit, peeled, seeded, and sectioned
  (remove membranes)

For the Roquefort Dressing:

½ pound Roquefort cheese
½ teaspoon salt
1 teaspoon dry mustard
dash cayenne pepper
1 teaspoon crushed garlic
1⅓ cups light olive oil
6 tablespoons tarragon vinegar at room temperature
6 tablespoons lemon juice
3 or 4 ice cubes
2 hard-boiled eggs, chopped

1. On each individual salad plate, make a bed of Boston lettuce. Put on top several pieces of fresh grapefruit. Cover with Roquefort Dressing.

2. To make the Roquefort Dressing, chop cheese in small pieces; combine in a medium bowl with salt, mustard, pepper, and garlic, and mix well with wooden salad fork or silver fork. Add oil slowly, mixing well. Add vinegar and lemon juice gradually; mix well.

3. Add ice cubes and stir gently until mixture thickens; remove what is left of ice cubes.

4. Stir in chopped eggs.

5. Put in covered jar and keep in refrigerator until ready to use.

8 servings (2 cups of dressing)

Country Ham

*A*llow yourself two days to make this ham just right.

½ country ham
(about 7–8 pounds)
4 ribs celery
1 large onion
4 sprigs parsley
10 whole cloves
2 teaspoons ground mace
or 2 blades mace

1¾ cups light brown sugar, divided
¼ cup fine dry bread crumbs
1 teaspoon dry mustard
2 tablespoons melted ham fat
3 cups sparkling cider

1. Ask the butcher to give you the half of the ham with the most meat on it. The night before cooking, wash ham thoroughly, scrape all over with knife, and place to soak in a large pot of cold water.

2. The next day, pour off water and rinse out pot. Put ham in the large pot with celery, onion, parsley, cloves, mace, and one cup of the sugar. Add enough cold water to cover ham. Bring to boil; reduce heat, cover, and simmer until tender, allowing about 25 minutes per pound. Remove from heat and allow ham to cool in liquid. When cool enough to handle, remove ham from pot and pull off skin. Place ham in large roasting pan. Preheat oven to 400°F.

3. In a large bowl, combine the remaining sugar, bread crumbs, mustard, and ham fat, and coat top of ham with this mixture. Pour sparkling cider around ham.

4. Put in oven and bake for about 25 minutes, basting occasionally.

5. Remove from oven, wrap in foil, and chill thoroughly (a hot ham does not slice well). Slice *very* thin.

Serves 10

Beaten Biscuits

Good beaten biscuits are also available at specialty stores. I give you this recipe for historical interest. Serve cold with country ham.

4 cups flour
1 teaspoon salt
¼ cup lard
½ cup ice water
½ cup cold milk

1. Preheat oven to 325°F.

2. In a medium bowl, combine flour and salt. Cut the lard into the flour with 2 knives or a pastry blender. Moisten dough alternately with ice water and milk until it is rather stiff.

3. Remove from bowl, put on floured board, and knead dough until smooth. Then beat or pound with a mallet, until dough blisters.

4. Roll dough out about ½-inch thick. Cut with a small biscuit cutter and prick each biscuit 3 times with a fork.

5. Bake in oven until lightly brown, about 30 minutes.

About 40 biscuits

Green Tomato Chutney

Published here for the first time, this secret recipe was given to me by a good friend. It is well worth the effort.

4 pounds tiny green tomatoes
1 pound green peppers
4 hot peppers, seeded
1 pound onions
½ pound celery
½ pound (1½ cups) golden seedless raisins
4 pounds dark brown sugar
1 pound crystallized ginger
1 bottle McCormick pickling spice
1 teaspoon powdered ginger
1 quart red wine vinegar
1 pound golden delicious apples

1. Chop all ingredients, except celery and apples, into 1-inch pieces. (Wear gloves when you cut up the hot peppers.) String celery and cut into very thin 1-inch strips. Tie spices in cheesecloth.

2. Put all ingredients except apples into a large kettle. Bring to boil, reduce heat to medium, and cook for 2 hours or more, depending on the amount of juice. The mixture should have a congealed consistency.

3. Peel and core apples, slice very thin, and add in the last ½ hour of cooking. Remove spices. Serve as a condiment with country ham, cold meat, or curry.

Makes about 7 pints

Henretta's Stewed Corn

One of Henretta's best dishes. I have tried to re-create it from memory.

> 12 ears tender young white corn
> 4 tablespoons butter
> 2 cups heavy cream
> salt
> pepper

1. With a small sharp knife, cut the rows of kernels in half. Cut off the tips of the kernels into a large bowl. Scrape the pulp from the cobs into the bowl.

2. Put corn and other ingredients into the top of a double boiler. Cover and cook over boiling water (medium heat) for three hours, stirring occasionally. Serve hot.

8 servings

Baby Lima Beans

A simple recipe that brings out the flavor of the beans.

> 2 pounds baby lima beans
> 2 tablespoons butter
> 1 teaspoon salt
> pepper
> 2 tablespoons heavy cream (optional)

1. Put beans in a medium pot, cover with water, bring to a boil, reduce heat and add butter and salt, and simmer until tender and water has evaporated, about 10–15 minutes.

2. Add pepper to taste and, if you like, a little cream, and simmer for a few additional minutes.

8 servings

My Mother's Yellow Squash Casserole

_M_y mother claims that she is not a cook, but sometimes she goes into the kitchen and produces something delicious like this.

> 2 pounds yellow summer squash, sliced
> 4 tablespoons butter
> 1 green pepper, chopped
> 1 large onion, chopped
> 4 tablespoons sour cream
> ½ cup grated sharp Cheddar cheese
> 1 cup bread crumbs, divided
> salt
> white pepper
> bits of butter

1. Cook squash in a large pot of gently boiling salted water for about 5 minutes, until crisp but tender. Drain.

2. Melt butter in a large, heavy skillet over medium-low heat. Cook green pepper and onion until onion is transparent, about 15 minutes. Be careful not to brown. Add drained squash and cook another 5 minutes. Add sour cream, cheese, and ½ cup of the bread crumbs. Add salt and white pepper to taste.

3. Transfer to an ovenproof 9-by-12-inch casserole and sprinkle with remaining bread crumbs. Dot with bits of butter. May be made ahead to this point.

4. Before serving, heat in 350°F oven for about 30 minutes, or until hot and bread crumbs are browned.

8 servings

Buttermilk Pie

*M*y mother says that this is Murlo's buttermilk pie as she remembers it.

For the Pie Crust:

1½ cups flour
¼ teaspoon salt
1 stick butter
¼ cup ice water

1. Preheat oven to 350°F.

2. In a medium bowl, combine flour and salt. Work butter into flour with two knives or pastry blender. Add ice water and blend well with a fork. Make into a ball and roll out on a floured surface into a 10-inch round. Place in a 9-inch pie pan. Prick with fork and bake for 7 to 8 minutes. Cool.

For the Filling:

3 eggs, separated
1⅓ cups sugar, divided
2 tablespoons cornstarch
pinch of salt
4 tablespoons melted butter
1 tablespoon lemon juice
½ teaspoon freshly grated nutmeg
1 cup buttermilk
¼ teaspoon cream of tartar

1. In a medium bowl, beat egg yolks with 1 cup of the sugar, cornstarch, and salt. Add butter, lemon juice, nutmeg, and buttermilk. Mix well.

2. Pour into prebaked pie shell and bake at 350°F for about 20 minutes, until custard is almost set.

3. Meanwhile, beat egg whites with an electric mixer until frothy; add cream of tartar. Gradually add remaining $\frac{1}{3}$ cup of sugar and continue beating until meringue stands up in stiff peaks.

4. Remove the partially baked pie from the oven and cover it with the meringue, making sure that it touches the crust all around. Return to oven and bake 5 to 10 more minutes, until top is browned. Allow to cool before serving.

8 servings

Miss Lady at finishing school

Divinity

WHEN SUSAN AND I were teenagers, a businessman from Atlanta bought one of the old houses in Greensboro and remodeled it as a retirement home. It was a big, rambling, white frame Victorian home about three blocks away from Miss Lady's, surrounded by old trees and spacious gardens that had lazily gone to seed during the illness that preceded Miss Louisa's death. Miss Louisa was a close friend of Miss Lady's and also a distant relative. Every summer, a few days after we arrived in Greensboro, Miss Lady would take Susan and me aside and say in her soft voice, which was nonetheless compelling, "Now girls, I hope you won't mind calling on some of my friends. It would mean the world to them, and the world to me." And bursting into tears, as if to preclude any excuses, "Let's start with Miss Louisa. Her life is *hard*." She managed to pronounce "hard" in three syllables— "ha-ah-rd"—so that it didn't sound so bad after all. We would go cheerfully off to Miss Louisa's. Her genteel poverty gave her house an air of shabby comfort and pleasing disorder. And authenticity: she never said that the old bullet lying on the table in the front hall had killed a Yankee general—no, it merely fell out of her father's hunting rifle one day when she was cleaning out the garage. Once when I called a thistle in her garden a "purple star," Miss Louisa said, "It's just a weed, honey."

Eveline Batts, the wife of the Atlanta businessman who bought Miss Louisa's house after her death, had visions of becoming Greensboro's grande dame, and she transformed the old place into what she considered to be an appropriate setting. The town talked when Miss Louisa's worn Victorian furniture with its horsehair upholstery was disposed of at a yard sale and the big moving vans from Atlanta rumbled up to the front door. The town talked even more when the cutting gardens, bubbling over with hardy summer flowers, were trans-formed into a formal "green garden" by a landscape architect from Charleston. And it was rumored that Mrs. Batts had oriental carpets on her kitchen floor.

Miss Lady was curious about what the inside of the house looked like, but she could not bring herself to accept one of the Batts's many invitations to visit. On one of her afternoon drives (LeRoy took her for a drive around town every afternoon after her nap), she saw a pile of old books and papers on the curb waiting to be hauled away. She took a bottle of cologne out of her purse, sprinkled her handkerchief, and pressed it mournfully against her temples. Her eyes filled with tears. "Those must be Louisa's father's law books," she said. "He passed the bar the year Mama and Papa married."

The Batts hired several kinds of help, more than they needed. Eveline Batts called one of the women who worked for her "the upstairs maid" and another one "the downstairs maid." Judge said she should get one for the back porch. The Batts wanted to be called Miss Eveline and Mr. Joe by their help and everyone else in Greensboro. Susan and I asked Miss Annie, Miss Lady's sister, what we should call them. "Call them Miss Eveline and Mr. Joe," she said. "Always do people the courtesy of accepting them as they think they are, not as you know them to be."

"'Mr. Joe' sure does sound funny," said Susan.

Finally, Miss Lady persuaded Judge to call on the Batts, since she could not go herself. Susan and I had heard so much of the town talk that we were almost as curious as Miss Lady. Judge said he would be glad to have our company. Miss Lady let us know, without seeming too eager, that she wanted a report full and complete in every detail.

Sunday afternoon at four o'clock the butler showed us into "the ladies' parlor," as opposed to "the gentlemen's parlor" across the hall. The room, simply furnished and uncluttered when Miss Louisa was alive, overflowed with what Judge called "doodads and folderol." The large windows were swathed in heavy fringed gold satin drapes tied back with tassels. I recognized the furniture (from having read one of Miss Lady's books on antiques) as eighteenth-century French. The keys in the chests of drawers and the secretary were decorated with pink satin bows. Heavy gilt frames displayed reproductions of sentimental nineteenth-century paintings.

Mr. Joe, stocky, with a florid face, stood to greet us. Miss Eveline, a large woman with pretty features, remained seated on a settee with the skirt of her printed voile "afternoon dress" spread carefully around her. She stretched out her arms to Susan and me, calling us "those two adorable Evans girls."

Miss Eveline felt that in order to become Greensboro's great lady she must always be sweet. Her manner was so delicate and sympathetic that people often thought something terrible had happened and she was afraid to break the news to them. (Judge called her "a mighty silly woman," but as time passed and he came to know her better, he decided that her delicacy was motivated by a genuine anxiety over hurting people's feelings.)

We heard a knock at the front door, and Mr. Joe said, "That's Brother Bill." The Batts were new members of Greensboro's Methodist church, and the preacher made his calls on Sunday afternoon.

Brother Bill appeared in the doorway. He was a big young man who wore a dark blue suit, a white shirt with a narrow black tie, and large, shiny black shoes. His lank brown hair was smoothed back from his forehead and he had combed it so carefully we could see the marks the comb had left. Brother Bill had been the recipient of the scholarship for ministry students that Judge and Miss Lady had established in memory of my father at a small Methodist college in north Georgia. He thought his career was off to a good start when he was assigned to the church in Greensboro, the church that had been built by Miss Lady's father.

He stood very straight in the doorway, holding a big plate covered with a gingham cloth. "Divinity," he explained, proffering the plate, made by his wife especially for Miss Eveline. (Divinity is an old-fashioned Southern candy, made with pecans, whipped egg whites, and sugar—lots of sugar.)

Miss Eveline received the platter from Brother Bill with gracious thanks and told Mr. Joe to pull the bell cord in the corner. "Call in the downstairs maid to pass Coca-Cola." Brother Bill, balancing himself on a tiny chair, sighed dramatically and said, "I declare."

Brother Bill was hoping that Miss Eveline (or Miss Lady) would contribute a silver communion service to the church. But he felt unprepared to navigate the subtleties of Greensboro etiquette, and he knew that the wrong word might offend her sensibilities. He decided to play it safe, as he always did when he called on Miss Lady. Every time something was said to which he did not know how to respond, he exclaimed, "Bless your heart," uttered with what he thought to be the right mixture of sacerdotal solemnity and sociable enthusiasm.

"This divinity is real good," said Miss Eveline. "Just about the best I ever tasted."

"Bless your heart," said Brother Bill.

"I do hope you like Coca-Cola," said Miss Eveline as the downstairs maid handed around the frosted glasses. "I think Coca-Cola goes real good with divinity. Do have another piece."

"After you," he said.

"I don't mind if I do," said Miss Eveline.

Mr. Joe was becoming restless. He shifted his weight around on his French chair, occasioning alarmed looks from Miss Eveline, who was afraid the delicate legs would give way. He stuck his thumbs behind the lapels of his white linen jacket and jutted out his chin. Judge's blue eyes were sparkling, the only sign of amusement visible in his face.

Miss Eveline, worried that the conversation was lagging, cast around for something appropriate to say.

"I just love to read the Bible," she said. "There are so many sweet stories in the Bible."

"Back then in Bible times," said Brother Bill, "they didn't have all the advantages we have now. As a matter of fact, when they took communion they just used an old jug and cup or something. They didn't have a silver communion service—"

"An old cup? The same old cup for everybody?" exclaimed Mr. Joe. "Phew-ee!"

Miss Eveline felt that Mr. Joe had overstepped the mark by saying "Phew-ee." "Thank goodness in *our* church," she said, "we each have our own little glass to drink out of." She tried to arrange a serene expression on her face. "I wonder what Jesus' friends called him," she said.

"I'll bet they called him Mr. Jesus," said Susan.

"Mr. Jesus? Honey, that doesn't sound quite right. I'll bet they called him Emmanuel. That sounds just right for Jesus. Emmanuel."

Brother Bill tried again. "Imagine someone named Emmanuel having to take communion out of an old jug. Now, if he had a big silver communion service—"

"Of course Jesus didn't have a big silver communion service," said Miss Eveline. "Jesus was *poor*."

"Bless your heart," said Brother Bill.

Judge said, "When Susan was a little girl, the first year she went to vacation Bible school, Miss Lady and I were real surprised when we looked at her coloring book. She colored Jesus' robe black and his hair red."

"For heaven's sake, child," said Miss Eveline, "Jesus' robe is *blue* and his hair is *blonde*!"

"Jesus strikes me as a redhead," said Susan.

"I see Jesus with blonde hair and a blue robe," said Brother Bill.

"Thank goodness we have preachers to set us straight," said Miss Eveline.

"Bless your heart," said Brother Bill. He turned to Susan and said crossly, "Miss Susan, I'm going to ask you a big question. Do you love God?"

Susan thought a moment, then replied, "I like him okay but I'm not wild about him."

Brother Bill took his leave, literally crestfallen—locks of his hair had fallen over his forehead—that the silver communion service had eluded him. No sooner was he out the door than Mr. Joe blew up at Miss Eveline.

"Don't be so damned sweet! That fellow probably thinks he has cancer and we're all afraid to tell him!"

"Mr. Joe," said Miss Eveline, "you are a hard man. You know my nerves can't take too much. I thought he would *never* leave. I don't want to hear anyone say 'Bless your heart' ever again. But I must say, his divinity is real good."

"You ate plenty of it," muttered Mr. Joe.

"I just couldn't hurt his feelings," said Miss Eveline. "Now you all just run along. I want to be by myself a little while. I'll just sit here on this settee and quiet my nerves. My nerves can't take too much."

So we left Miss Eveline in the parlor sitting in the same position in which we had first seen her, with her afternoon dress spread out around her. Mr. Joe told us good-bye in the hall, swore under his breath, and let the back door slam. We heard him call Merci Beaucoup, his bull terrier, as the butler showed us out.

That evening, Judge was deliberately silent about the afternoon's events, teasing Miss Lady. We were sitting on the front porch in our rocking chairs, waiting for Henretta to call us to supper. Miss Lady tried to make conversation, tried to show us that Miss Eveline and Mr. Joe were not the *only* things on her mind. Finally, she gave up.

"Well, Judge," she said, "how was it?"

Judge, with a straight face and laughing eyes, looked at Miss Lady and let his silence draw out to a long conclusion: "It was mighty flambooant."

"What happened?" asked Miss Lady.

"It was a mighty flambooant occasion."

"Is that all you have to say on the subject?"

"That's all I have to say on the subject."

"I declare, Judge, I wish you could be a little more—effusive."

Supper that evening was special, as if Henretta thought we needed real nourishment after spending the afternoon with "those folks." Miss Lady didn't savor the meal in her usual leisurely way, but ate quickly. Judge seemed to linger over every mouthful and said he was glad he lived in a house where people knew how things should taste. Miss Lady waited for him to elaborate, but Judge said no more.

After supper, when Judge had gone to bed, Miss Lady coaxed the details out of Susan and me. Her expression grew more astonished and delighted as we described the gold satin drapes, the French furniture ("in an unpretentious Victorian house," she said disapprovingly), the pink satin bows, the "paintings," the scene Mr. Joe made.

Miss Lady laughed until she cried, then caught herself up, realizing that she was perhaps setting a bad example. She wanted to teach us that it was unkind to be judgmental and make fun of people behind their backs.

"I am obliged to say that Miss Eveline and Mr. Joe are common. But they may have *hidden qualities* not readily apparent to the casual observer."

"They don't have enough hidden qualities to buy a silver communion service for the church," said Susan.

"How right you are, darling," said Miss Lady. Then, she added with a wicked little smile, "I guess we'll have to take communion out of an old jug, just like Jesus."

As the years passed, Judge and Miss Lady became friends with Miss Eveline and Mr. Joe. Judge said that although they were "mighty flambooant" they were "nice folks." They became involved in the Greensboro Cemetery Association and were largely responsible for saving the old cemetery in which Greensboro's first settlers, among them some of our ancestors, were buried. This endeared them to Miss Lady, who began to refer to them as her "good neighbors." Miss Eveline and Mr. Joe spent their money with an almost childish delight and were generous in giving it away. Their bad taste got on my nerves, and I tended to see them, when I first knew them, as shallow, farcical characters. But gradually I came to agree with Miss Lady and Judge, who discerned, behind their show of gold satin and gilt, warmth of heart and a desire to please and belong in Greensboro. Susan didn't say much about what she thought. Miss Eveline said of Susan, "That little blonde girl sitting on the sofa makes me nervous. She can see right through me."

Miss Lady eventually did give the church a silver communion service. I thought that a silver service called for wine at communion, and I was distressed that the Methodists served grape juice instead. But Susan said, "I like grape juice in an old jug."

Menu VI:

The supper Henretta gave us the day we visited the Batts.

❧

Chestnut Soup

Chicken with Tomatoes and Avocados

Elizabeth's Green Beans Charleston

Cheese Biscuits

Trifle

Chestnut Soup

A wonderful, warming soup. Canned chestnut puree is available at specialty stores.

        1 pound unsweetened chestnut puree
        4 cups chicken stock
        ½ cup chopped celery
        1 teaspoon chopped onion
        1 sprig thyme
        1 bay leaf
        ¼ teaspoon ground allspice
        ¼ teaspoon ground cloves
        1 teaspoon paprika
        2 tablespoons butter
        2 tablespoons flour
        1 cup heavy cream
        1 cup milk

1. In a soup pot, place the chestnut puree, chicken stock, celery, onion, herbs, and spices. Bring to boil, reduce heat, and simmer over low heat for 45 minutes.

2. In a small saucepan, melt the butter, add the flour, and cook this roux 3 minutes over low heat. Add ½ cup of the hot soup to roux, then add this mixture to the soup. Simmer for 2 to 3 minutes to thicken the soup.

3. Remove the sprig of thyme and the bay leaf, and puree the soup in a blender or food processor. Return soup to the pot.

4. Just before serving, add the cream and milk. Heat through, but do not let the soup boil.

8–10 servings

Chicken with Tomatoes and Avocados

This is adapted from a dish that Judge and Miss Lady sometimes ate at Antoine's.

    ¼ cup olive oil
    4 to 6 whole chicken breasts, halved, skinned, boned
    3 tablespoons butter
    9 large ripe tomatoes (or 11 medium), peeled, seeded, chopped
    1 teaspoon salt
    ⅛ teaspoon black pepper
    ⅛ teaspoon cayenne pepper
    1 sprig thyme or
       ¼ teaspoon rubbed thyme
    1 tablespoon minced fresh parsley
    1 bay leaf
    3 cloves garlic, finely minced
    1 tablespoon butter
    1 tablespoon flour
    6 shallots, finely minced
    1 large green pepper, finely chopped
    ½ cup white wine
    3 avocados, sliced

1. Heat the olive oil in a large skillet and sauté the chicken breasts over medium-high heat until browned on both sides. Remove from skillet and keep warm.

2. In a large casserole, melt 3 tablespoons butter. Add tomatoes and cook over low heat for 10 minutes. Add the salt, black pepper, and cayenne pepper. Cook over low heat for 10 minutes. Add the thyme, parsley, bay leaf, and garlic. Cook for 15 minutes.

3. Meanwhile, in a small saucepan, melt 1 tablespoon butter. Add 1 tablespoon flour, and cook roux for a few minutes over medium heat until brown. Add the shallots and the green pepper, and brown lightly. Add the white wine and cook over low heat until thick.

4. Add the shallots and green pepper mixture to the tomatoes, then add the chicken. Cover and cook over low heat for about 45 minutes, until the chicken is tender.

5. After the chicken is cooked, cut the meat into small pieces, then return to sauce. Serve hot on slices of avocado.

8 servings

Elizabeth's Green Beans Charleston

*M*y friend Elizabeth is a beautiful Charleston lady who knows all the culinary secrets of her city.

>2 pounds green beans (young tender
>   ones if possible), washed and trimmed
>6 tablespoons butter
>2 small onions, thinly sliced
>1 large clove garlic
>½ teaspoon salt
>2 tablespoons sesame seeds
>8 tablespoons chopped fresh parsley

1. In a large pot, bring 3 quarts of salted water to a boil. Add beans. Reduce heat and simmer beans until just tender, about 15–20 minutes. Drain and set aside.

2. Melt butter in a large skillet. Add onions and stir constantly over medium heat for 1 minute. Crush garlic and add to onions. Add beans and toss lightly over medium heat until coated with butter.

3. Meanwhile, toast sesame seeds in 350°F oven for about 5 minutes, being careful not to burn them.

4. Add sesame seeds and parsley to green beans, toss lightly, and serve at once.

8 servings

Cheese Biscuits

These should be served with the Chestnut Soup as well as the chicken.

> 1 stick butter, softened
> 1 cup grated sharp Cheddar cheese
> 1⅓ cups flour
> ½ teaspoon salt
> pinch of paprika
> pinch of cayenne pepper

1. Preheat oven to 375°F.

2. In a medium bowl, mix the butter, grated cheese, flour, and salt. Add the paprika and cayenne. Mix well with a wooden spoon. Form into a ball.

3. Roll out on a floured board to a thickness of about ¼ inch. Cut into small rounds.

4. Place on a baking sheet and cook about 10 minutes in oven. May be served hot or cold.

About 20 biscuits

Trifle

My favorite recipe in the book! For a festive dessert party, you may double the recipe and serve it with demitasse.

½ cup chopped pecans
½ cup golden seedless raisins
½ cup blackberry brandy
8 egg whites
pinch of salt
1½ cups sugar

1 teaspoon vanilla
1 cup heavy cream, whipped and lightly sweetened with a little sugar and the blackberry brandy in which the raisins and pecans have soaked

1. Mix the raisins and pecans in a small bowl, and pour the blackberry brandy over them. Let soak overnight.

2. Preheat oven to 250°F.

3. In a large bowl, beat the egg whites with the pinch of salt until stiff. Gradually beat in the sugar, then add the vanilla.

4. Drain the raisins and pecans, and reserve the liquid. Incorporate the raisins and pecans into the egg whites with a spatula.

5. Pour into a large, round, deep 10-inch cake mold or other large pan (the meringue will rise a lot).

6. Bake in oven for about 1 hour. Turn off the oven and allow the meringue to cool in the oven.

7. Unmold on a large platter or cake plate, and chill.

8. When ready to serve, ice with whipped cream flavored with a little sugar and the reserved blackberry brandy. (This makes a soft meringue.)

8 servings

Aunt Clare

The Rude
and Bleeding
Beet

ROUGHT UP BY Murlo and Miss Lady in the tradition
of Southern gentlewomen to create beauty, my sister and I had an ideal model
during our childhood—Murlo's sister, our great-aunt, whom we called Aunt
Clare. In her sixties, when we knew her, Aunt Clare was truly lovely. In fact,
some people called her "Lovely," and this inspired Susan and me, more thoroughly than any grown-up admonitions, to try to be like Aunt Clare. She was
tall like all the women in Murlo's family, with elegant arms and legs, delicate
hands and feet, dark eyebrows, and naturally wavy, brilliant white hair; her
carriage was erect and her voice musical and lilting. She never seemed stud-
ied—on the contrary, her grace seemed natural and her charm spontaneous. I
have a friend who says that there is no such thing as a naturally beautiful or
charming woman—some women are just more clever than others. If that's
true, our Aunt Clare was exceedingly clever.

Aunt Clare stayed with my mother, Murlo, Susan, and me in Nashville when she wasn't living in her native Little Rock. Her husband, Uncle Hiram, was a sweet-natured man who had found his purpose in life: to provide his wife with a luxurious home, servants, clothes from New York and Paris, and a touring car to take her away when Little Rock became boring. My mother disliked seeing a man manipulated by feminine charm and said, "Aunt Clare is the toast of Little Rock and Uncle Hiram is the milktoast of Little Rock."

Although Aunt Clare was sweet-tempered and loving, she was not democratic—she expected to be recognized as a great beauty and as such, to receive her due. She seemed always to have two porters hovering at her elbow, ready to pick up her steamer trunk and her hat box. Once when she visited in Greensboro she said curtly to my nurse, "Alberta, carry my bags upstairs." Alberta replied that she had been hired to be Miss Luann's nurse and that she wasn't obliged to take care of anybody but Miss Luann. Aunt Clare was stunned. This may have been the first time anyone had said no to her.

Aunt Clare could not have children, which deeply saddened her, but she was not resentful of other women. She was generous to her nieces and nephews, and in fact spent so much of her money on them that when she died there was very little left. She devoted herself full time to elegance, and she passed on her knowledge and taste to Susan and me. We would spend hours choosing material for a dress, turning it this way and that way in the light, deciding where the ribbons and lace should go. Aunt Clare knew how to draft a pattern from measurements and consequently could make her own designs. She always took our ideas seriously, and there was always enough material left over for a doll dress.

Though we would have been restless with anyone else, we would stand patiently while Aunt Clare fitted us. As she worked, she would make casual but compelling remarks about the way a beautiful woman carried herself, how she would conduct herself on such and such an occasion, how important it was to eat fresh fruit and drink very little alcohol (only wine) and to brush her hair one hundred strokes a day. When I was eleven she stood me in front of the full-length mirror in Murlo's room. She looked at me in my slip, then at my reflection in the mirror. She put her hands on her hips. "You are short-waisted," she said. "Every day you must put your hands on your hips, stretch up, and pull down with your hands. A truly beautiful woman is long-waisted."

Aunt Clare put on a magnificent, long dressing gown after she got up every morning. It was made of purple silk velvet, lined with mauve taffeta. I still have this dressing gown; the pile of the velvet is so thick that even after all these years it has not crushed or worn. My husband, an actor, once wore it to play Macbeth. It seemed to fit the dark princeliness of the character. But Aunt Clare was all innocence when she wore the purple velvet dressing gown. Breakfasting on fruit and tea, smelling of her flowery and subtle cologne, she seemed to promise that the day ahead would be interesting and full of romance. Susan and I would trudge off to school knowing that when we returned in the afternoon we could exchange our saddle oxfords and woolen jumpers for Aunt Clare's satin slippers and silky dresses to play at going to an evening party.

Aunt Clare was with us during the ice storm of 1951. Winters in Nashville are usually mild, with much warm weather and rain. But occasionally the temperature will drop sharply, all the water-laden trees suddenly become heavy with ice, and a snowstorm paralyzes the city. Nashville was completely unprepared for real winters and had no equipment to clear or salt the roads. For ten days all the electric and telephone lines went down, the water pipes froze, and the city services collapsed. My mother heated the house with the gas stove in the kitchen and the fireplaces in the living room and bedrooms. Wood had to be hauled in from the back porch and groceries carried several blocks over icy sidewalks.

Murlo, used to trouble and indeed rather surprised when it *didn't* come, was grim and determined to defeat the weather, as she had defeated so many other of life's adversities. She stacked wood, laid fires, carried out ashes, and shoveled snow off the walks. Meanwhile, Aunt Clare spent the duration of the ice storm dressed in her purple velvet dressing gown, playing pioneer with Susan and me. We huddled cosily around the fireplace in our bedroom, boiling milk and tea and toasting bread on forks, trying to outdo each other in imagining dangerous, but glamorous, Western adventures. Aunt Clare was transformed into the most stunning cowgirl who ever rode a wild horse. Susan and I imagined that her saddle (a sidesaddle, of course) was studded with turquoise and silver and her boots were made of fawn-colored suede. She became friendly with the Indians even though they scalped everyone else in her party (who would dare scalp Aunt Clare?), and she cured a little Indian boy of pneumonia by wrapping him in her purple velvet dressing gown. I said that I would make coffee over the campfire by throwing some coffee grounds into a pot of boiling water, then tossing in a crushed eggshell (a recipe from one of my cowgirl books). But Aunt Clare said that this was not the proper way to make coffee. She pretended to telegraph Uncle Hiram back in Little Rock, who immediately sent by pony express a cannister of mocha-java, a percolator, and a porcelain coffee service.

My mother (as she told me later) was extremely anxious during the storm. She was responsible for feeding and keeping warm five people, two of whom were elderly women, and she worried that if they had heart attacks, there would be no way of getting them to a hospital. My mother took a dim view of Aunt Clare in her purple velvet dressing gown, but she knew as well as everyone else that Aunt Clare couldn't haul wood. It would be like asking Miss Lady to mop the kitchen floor; it was unthinkable. Did Aunt Clare possess that maddening innocence, that inviolable sense of security that pampered people often have? Or did she know that by keeping Susan and me too occupied to be frightened she was making her contribution? My mother thinks the former, but I tend to give Aunt Clare credit for the latter.

Aunt Clare's old clothes were packed in trunks in the attic. I spent many rainy afternoons dressing up in these cast-offs. Pale pink and green oriental silk shawls, embroidered with birds and flowers that were as bright as my daydreams, with fringe a foot long that swayed and rippled like water. A serpentine black velvet evening dress that made me want to abandon my childhood and become a woman so that I could wear black and go out in the evening. Summer dresses of cream-colored or pastel linen trimmed with ruching and mother-of-pearl buttons. If Aunt Clare and Uncle Hiram should ever take me with them to New York, I thought, I would wear such a dress when we went to the Plaza for tea. I would enter the Palm Court just as Aunt Clare would—simply, never calling attention to myself, but so graceful as I walked across the room in my swaying skirt that everyone would notice.

Aunt Clare died many years ago. Her artful beauty now seems as superfluous and old-fashioned as a black lace fan. But I can't forget her. All through college, I worked very hard and I didn't have many dates. I spent most of my time and energy studying French and English literature. But if I was asked out for the evening, I would pin up my hair and put on a dinner dress. I would serenely face the bewildered young man across the table, trying to be lithesome and long-waisted, trying to be a beautiful woman.

My husband and I married soon after graduation. One summer we drove through Greece in a Volkswagen, sleeping in youth hostels, eating bread and cheese by the side of the road to save money. But I packed a brocade evening dress in my suitcase—one never knows when one might need a brocade evening dress.

Aunt Clare never did much cooking, but sometimes she would go into the kitchen and produce something special. It was always an occasion when she made beets in orange sauce. The kitchen was no longer a dull room at the back of the house but a corridor of anticipation, a scene of creation. She would cut the tops off the unpromising brown beets, cook them in boiling water until their sanguine juices stained the pan, and peel them, making a mess at the kitchen table. Somehow, Aunt Clare's mess was not as slovenly as other peoples', and she always brought off without a blunder the delicate sauce. She transfigured the rude and bleeding beet—doing what she did best—cutting reality to a crystal of romance.

Menu VII:

I remember the time Aunt Clare made her beets
alongside Cousin Catherine's Chicken—it was
delicious, and beautiful to behold.

Crab Soup

Cousin Catherine's Chicken Vermouth
with Walnuts and Green Grapes

Beets in Orange and Ginger Sauce

Old-Fashioned Caramel Ice Cream

Lemon Wafers

Crab Soup

A rich soup. Serve in small portions.

> 2 sticks butter
> ½ cup finely chopped green onions,
>   white part only
> 2 tablespoons flour
> 1 lemon, sliced, seeded (with rind)
> 4 cups light cream (half and half)
> 1 pound crab meat (be sure all shell is
>   removed from the crab meat)
> ½ teaspoon salt
> ¼ teaspoon white pepper
> Tabasco sauce to taste
> ½ cup cream sherry
> fresh parsley, chopped

1. In a large, heavy saucepan, melt the butter over low heat and add the green onions. Cook for one minute and stir in the flour. Cook roux 2 minutes over low heat, blending with a wooden spoon. Add the sliced, seeded lemon and, gradually, the cream. Stir the mixture until smooth. Let simmer over low heat for 5 minutes.

2. Add the crab meat, salt, white pepper, Tabasco sauce, and sherry, and heat through. Serve in heated bowls and sprinkle with a little parsley.

8 servings

Cousin Catherine's Chicken Vermouth with Walnuts and Green Grapes

Catherine was not only my cousin but also a good friend. She gave me this recipe during one of my visits to her home in Atlanta.

> 3 chicken breasts, halved
> 3 tablespoons flour
> salt
> pepper
> dried or finely minced fresh herbs: parsley,
>   tarragon, marjoram, dill, etc.
> ½ stick butter
> ½ pound mushrooms, sliced
> ¾ cup dry white vermouth
> 1 cup green seedless grapes, halved
> ¼ cup walnuts

1. Preheat oven to 300°F.

2. Combine flour, salt, pepper, and herbs in a paper or plastic bag; put chicken in bag one piece at a time, and shake it, coating chicken with flour and seasonings; shake off excess.

3. Melt butter in a large heavy skillet. Sauté chicken over medium-high heat on both sides for several minutes until golden brown. Remove from skillet and keep warm in a large casserole.

4. Sauté mushrooms in skillet, adding more butter if necessary.
   Add mushrooms to chicken in casserole.

5. Add vermouth to skillet. Cook over low heat for 3 or 4 minutes,
   mingling pan scrapings with vermouth.

6. Sprinkle grapes and walnuts over chicken and mushrooms.
   Pour vermouth over.

7. Cover the casserole and cook in oven for 30 minutes. Serve with rice.

6 servings

Beets in Orange and Ginger Sauce

The deep red color of this dish seems so appropriate for Aunt Clare.

1½ pounds beets
2 tablespoons butter
2 tablespoons flour
½ cup water
1 cup fresh orange juice
3 teaspoons grated orange rind
4½ tablespoons light brown sugar
½ teaspoon ground ginger
½ teaspoon curry powder
salt
2 heaping tablespoons crystallized ginger, chopped

1. Cut off tops of beets, put beets in large saucepan, and cover with water. Boil them until tender, about 30 to 40 minutes, or longer for older beets. Drain.

2. Melt butter in a large saucepan, add flour, and cook roux over low heat for 2 to 3 minutes (do not brown); add water and orange juice, stirring constantly. Add orange rind, brown sugar, ground ginger, and curry powder. Season with salt to taste. Remove from heat. Add crystallized ginger.

3. Peel and slice beets thinly and add to sauce. Make a few hours in advance to let beets marinate in sauce. Serve hot.

6 servings

Old-Fashioned Caramel Ice Cream

*S*weet and creamy, this is nicely balanced when served with lemon wafers on the side.

    3 cups sugar, divided
    8 tablespoons water
    6 eggs, slightly beaten
    pinch of salt
    4 cups heavy cream
    4 cups heavy cream, half-whipped
    3 teaspoons vanilla
    toasted pecans, coarsely chopped

1. Caramelize 2 cups of the sugar by combining it with 8 tablespoons water in a large, heavy sauce pan and boiling it over medium-high heat until nut brown; this will take 5 to 7 minutes. Keep warm.

2. In a large, heavy saucepan, combine the beaten eggs, the remaining 1 cup sugar, a pinch of salt, and unwhipped cream. Cook over very low heat, stirring constantly until the custard has thickened (160°F on a candy thermometer). Add the caramelized sugar while custard is hot, and stir to dissolve the sugar. Cool to room temperature. Add vanilla and the half-whipped cream. Freeze in an ice cream freezer according to manufacturer's directions. Serve with pecans sprinkled on top.

2 quarts

Lemon Wafers

*A*n easy, light sugar cookie.

> ½ teaspoon grated lemon peel
> ½ cup sugar
> 1 stick butter
> ¾ cup flour, sifted
> 1 egg
> ½ teaspoon vanilla
> pinch of salt

1. Preheat oven to 350°F.

2. In a medium bowl, mash the grated lemon peel into the sugar.

3. Beat the butter and sugar together until light and fluffy. Beat in the egg, flour, and vanilla.

4. Drop by teaspoonfuls onto a buttered baking sheet. Bake until golden brown, about 8 minutes.

2 dozen wafers

Miss Lady and Judge at the time of their marriage

Yellow Roses

*M*Y GREAT-GRANDFATHER, Edward Copeland, Miss Lady's father, had made my family's life in Greensboro possible. A self-made man born in a log cabin without formal education, he came to Greensboro in the 1880s to make his fortune. In a few years he established a bank and a cotton mill in the town and acquired extensive holdings in Greene County and Atlanta. My great-grandmother, Leila Davis, came from a proud old Georgia family impoverished by the Civil War. The beautiful things Edward Copeland brought back from his travels and gave to her, the house he built for her, his election to the state senate, his kindness to the people who worked for him— Miss Lady said that these were offerings to his wife, his tribute to an extraordinary love.

Miss Lady kept her father's obituary, published in the Atlanta papers, in one of her scrapbooks and showed it to me often when I was growing up. It was written by a friend of Edward Copeland's who had known him as a young man. After an absence of twenty years, he met Edward Copeland again and was exceedingly impressed: "the golden-hearted gentleman was the same as of yore." Judge said that this was mighty fancy talk, but Miss Lady was at pains to impress upon me that my great-grandfather was indeed a golden-hearted gentleman and my great-grandmother a beautiful and accomplished lady. They were vivid presences in my life—I lived in their house, with their furniture, their flowers, their porcelain, their pictures, and their recipes.

The parlor was an important room in this house. Here, Miss Lady kept her scrapbooks, family heirlooms, and many family photographs. To me, the most fascinating object in the parlor was a valentine sent by Alexander Stephens, vice-president of the Confederacy, to Judge's grandmother, Frances Cobb.

My great-great-grandmother and Alexander Stephens lived on adjoining plantations in Crawfordville, Georgia, not far from Greensboro. I liked to imagine that they were in love with each other. But Judge pointed out that this would have been impossible, considering their respective ages. Stephens was a middle-aged man and Frances Cobb a little girl when they wrote to each other. According to Miss Lady, they exchanged many letters, but the only surviving piece of correspondence was the valentine. Miss Lady had had the valentine, along with its brown paper envelope (addressed in Stephens's elegant handwriting), mounted on crushed blue velvet and framed in gold. She would often point it out to Susan and me and try to impress upon us that Alexander Stephens was a great man, "the best mind in the Confederate government," Judge said.

I was disappointed that Frances Cobb and Alexander Stephens had not been lovers. But Judge said that the true facts of their story were more interesting than the ones I imagined. He said that Stephens was a man of brilliant intellect and irreproachable integrity but that he was physically deformed and always ill. He never married. As the circumstances of his life became more difficult, his mental and moral faculties became more powerful. Judge showed me a passage from one of his letters: "The secret of my life has been revenge. . . . Not revenge in the usual acceptation of that term—but a determination to war over against fate—to meet the world in all its forces, to master evil with good. . . . My greatest courage has been drawn from the deepest despair."

I couldn't imagine such a man sending a valentine to a little girl, but Judge could. He could imagine it, he said, very well.

I think often of the valentine that was such a presence in my childhood. It hung in a quiet corner of the parlor, next to a window that gave onto the front porch. The cream-colored paper was bordered with cream-colored lace, and in the left-hand corner was a picture of a slender, black-haired young woman in a green dress, one hand against her cheek, the other resting in her lap. She was surrounded by a wreath of pink roses with gold leaves mingled among the green.

THE SEPTEMBER I was seventeen, to celebrate my going away to college, Miss Lady served champagne one evening before a supper that Henretta made an effort to turn into a special occasion. Judge and Miss Lady and I gathered in the parlor, and Henretta handed round the champagne in little crystal and gold cups and saucers (champagne was often served in cups in the old South). I wondered if Edward Copeland and Leila Davis had bought them on their wedding trip to New Orleans, but Miss Lady said no, Leila Davis had inherited them from her mother.

"Try to stick to the truth," said Judge.

Miss Lady said, "If you start with plain fact, it doesn't hurt to add a little fancy embroidery. It is true that Papa gave Mama a Rolls-Royce for their thirtieth wedding anniversary. And because she loved yellow roses, he saw to it that there was always a vase of yellow roses on her dressing table."

"Only when roses were in season," said Judge. "Not even Edward Copeland could produce roses in December."

"Where did they stay in New Orleans?" I asked Miss Lady.

"Such a long time ago," she said. "You don't really expect me to remember, do you?"

"Just go ahead and make something up," said Judge.

"Mama and Papa married over the objections of her family," said Miss Lady, ignoring him. "The Davises were proud. Proud of their ancestors. Proud of the money they no longer had. Edward Copeland wasn't good enough for them. But they were wrong. Papa was a gentleman. He enabled them to keep their home. As you know, the big house is Judge's family home, but for several years the Davises lived there. Papa was good to them and he was unassuming about it. He never rubbed it in that they were poor and he was rich. And such a life he gave Mama! Not many women are so deeply loved."

I looked at the portraits of Edward Copeland and Leila Davis [photographs taken just before they married] placed next to each other on the console table. Her face is serene and beautiful, with black hair smoothed back from her brow and large, untroubled, luminous eyes. His face is quick with intelligence and energy.

In the big house after the Civil War, Leila grew up cautiously and mournfully, with people who were old, who had lost. They confined themselves to one room in the winter because they could not afford to heat the whole house. They gathered for their table the few vegetables and flowers their untended garden produced. They maintained toward one another a courtesy that was scrupulous and sorrowful, trying to remember something that seemed further and further away, "the time before the War." Poverty gnawed at their hearts and subverted their confidence in life.

Leila was carefully brought up, perhaps more carefully than if her family had been prosperous. Her mammy, Sarah, mended and "turned" her clothes, dressed her hair, insisted she practice piano and learn French. She was prepared for a life that it looked like she might never have. But when she accepted Edward Copeland's proposal, her parents forbade the marriage. When Leila insisted hysterically that she *would* marry Edward Copeland, her mother locked her in the closet of her bedroom. Sarah unlocked the closet. Edward and Leila eloped.

When I visited the big house I would sometimes linger upstairs in Leila's bedroom, telling myself her story. I imagined that very little had been changed in the room since she left it: The tester bed with its slender posts, the crocheted lace canopy carefully laundered and arranged on the frame so the holes wouldn't show. The handwoven cream-colored bedspread painstakingly mended and patched to preserve the pattern of willow branches. One small rug, far too small to make warm and welcoming the expanse of cold floorboards—a little oriental placed by the side of the bed so Leila would not have to put her bare feet on the floor when she got out of bed in the morning. A tall, narrow chest of drawers. A stiff little maple rocker with a hard woven rush seat, so different from the carved rosewood furniture upholstered in velvet and damask with which Edward Copeland would fill their house. And the closet—a white door against a white wall, a glass doorknob, a brass lock with an iron key.

Miss Lady saw me looking at the two portraits on the console table. "Mama and I always dressed up for Papa because he appreciated all the details. When we went to Paris together in 1903, I took a trunk and a hat with pink plumes."

I imagined Edward Copeland walking down the Avenue de l'Opéra, wife on one arm, daughter on the other. Miss Lady's pink plumes rise and fall with the rhythm of their progress. Leila Davis, very slender, very straight, her face no longer young but still beautiful, wears flowers in her hair. Are they yellow roses?

Menu VIII:

My going-away-to-college celebration dinner.

❧

Molded Roquefort Cheese Ring

Stuffed Loin of Veal

Green Peas
with Mint and Cream

Ginger Sherbet
with Whipped Cream

Molded Roquefort Cheese Ring

*T*his is an appetizer that may also be served as a light lunch. Accompany this meal with Leslie's Southern French Bread (page 37).

6 ounces cream cheese, at room temperature
3 ounces Roquefort cheese, at room temperature
¾ cup milk
1 envelope gelatin
3 tablespoons cold water
½ teaspoon salt
1 tablespoon lemon juice
½ cup pecans, chopped
½ cup heavy cream, whipped

1. In a large bowl, blend cream cheese and Roquefort cheese together with wooden spoon until soft; add milk and mix well.

2. In a small bowl, soften gelatin in cold water, then melt it by placing it over hot water for a few minutes. Slowly add gelatin to cheese mixture, stirring well. Add salt, lemon juice, and nuts. Delicately fold in whipped cream.

3. Rinse out a shallow 10-inch ring mold with cold water, shake out excess, and pour in mixture. Cover and refrigerate until set.

4. Unmold on a platter and garnish with lettuce leaves and, if you wish, radishes cut to look like roses.

6 small servings

Stuffed Loin of Veal

$\mathcal{A}$ star entrée for an important meal. I like to swirl a few tablespoons of pear preserves into the gravy before serving.

½ pound lean veal, ground
¼ pound pork, ground
½ cup soft bread crumbs
2 teaspoons finely chopped
   fresh parsley
2 teaspoons finely chopped onion
½ teaspoon grated lemon rind
1 slice garlic clove, chopped
salt, pepper, rubbed thyme,
   ground cloves, ground nutmeg
1 egg, slightly beaten
2 tablespoons sherry

1 4-pound veal rump roast, boned,
   with a cavity sliced into it for stuffing
6 bacon slices
2 medium onions, sliced
2 cups veal or chicken stock
1 bouquet garni (2 parsley sprigs,
   1 bay leaf, sprig of thyme or
   ¼ teaspoon rubbed thyme,
   and peeled garlic clove)
10 peppercorns
fresh watercress and gherkins
2 tablespoons pear preserves (optional)

1. In a large bowl, mix together the ground veal, pork, bread crumbs, parsley, onion, lemon rind, and garlic. Sprinkle lightly with salt, pepper, thyme, cloves, and nutmeg. Stir in egg and sherry.

2. Fill cavity of veal roast with stuffing. Secure opening by tying roast firmly with twine.

3. Place in a deep kettle and cover with bacon and onion slices. Pour in stock, add bouquet garni and peppercorns. Bring to boil, reduce heat, and simmer for 2½ hours, or until tender, turning meat several times.

4. Remove meat from kettle, remove twine from meat, and keep meat warm in oven.

5. Strain stock into saucepan and boil rapidly until reduced to a glaze.

6. Slice meat carefully and arrange on warm serving platter. Coat with sauce and garnish with watercress and gherkins.

6 servings

Green Peas with Mint and Cream

The best way to serve fresh peas.

> 1 ½ pounds tiny green peas
> 2 cups water
> 3 tablespoons butter
> the white part of 3 green onions, finely chopped
> ½ cup heavy cream
> ½ teaspoon sugar
> salt
> 1 handful fresh mint leaves, chopped
> 2 tablespoons fresh parsley, finely chopped

1. In a medium pot, bring 2 cups water to boil. Add the peas, reduce heat, and simmer until they are just tender, about 5–10 minutes. Drain.

2. Melt the butter in a large skillet. Add the onions and cook over low heat until they are transparent, about 10 minutes. Add the peas, cream, sugar, and salt. Keep hot.

3. Just before serving, add the parsley and mint. Toss lightly. Serve immediately.

6 servings

Ginger Sherbet with Whipped Cream

The ginger flavor provides just the right amount of spiciness to this light sherbet.

> 3 oranges
> 4 lemons
> 1 quart water
> 2 ½ cups sugar
> 1 ½ cups dry white wine
> 6 ounces preserved ginger (with its syrup)
> 1 pint heavy cream, whipped, unsweetened

1. Pare thin rinds of oranges and 3 of the lemons with carrot scraper or small knife. Put peel in a large pot with water and sugar. Boil over high heat until it makes a syrup (230°F on candy thermometer). Cool. Strain off fruit peel and discard, reserving syrup.

2. Squeeze juice from 3 oranges and 4 lemons, and add to cool syrup, along with white wine. Put this mixture in freezer of refrigerator for several hours.

3. Puree preserved ginger with its syrup in blender or food processor.

4. When fruit juice mixture is half-frozen, remove from freezer and beat with electric mixer, adding pureed ginger. Return this mixture to freezer and finish freezing (overnight).

5. Serve in sherbet glasses with unsweetened whipped cream.

1 ½ quarts of sherbet

Getting ready for a trip to Atlanta

*One for the
Cutworm,
One for the
Crow*

WHEN I WAS seventeen, I won scholarships to Radcliffe and to Agnes Scott, a women's college in Atlanta. Although Miss Lady and Judge didn't say so explicitly, I knew they wanted me to go to Agnes Scott. They thought I was too young to go far away from home. Of course, I wanted to go to Radcliffe, and my mother supported me. Her family had been unable to send her to college during the Depression, and she wanted me to have the best education I could get. If Murlo had been alive at the time she, too, would have thrown her weight behind Radcliffe. A few days after I heard that I had been accepted by Radcliffe, a letter arrived from Greensboro:

Dear Luann,

I hear that you plan to attend Radcliffe College. Be careful and go slow.

Love, Judge

The first week in September, Judge, Miss Lady, my mother, and Susan put me on the train in Atlanta. Judge gave the porter ten dollars and told him to take care of me. The porter put my luggage on the rack and I settled myself in the Pullman seat. The train began to move. Looking out the window, I saw slipping away from me the four beloved people I so much wanted to leave. Judge, more stooped than usual, worried that I would not come back, or that I'd come back so changed I would never again fit into his world. Miss Lady wept, not wanting to let me go but at the same time proud of me, perhaps realizing the possibility of a transformation of my life as a woman that she would never have admitted for herself. My mother smiled radiantly, waving good-bye with her strong arms, as if trying to infuse me with her own courage.

The train pulled smoothly out of the station. I could no longer see them. The sadness I felt quickly passed away, almost as soon as I lost sight of their upturned, anxious faces. I didn't know what it meant to be left behind. I was setting out on a voyage that was bound to end in happiness and fulfillment. Optimism, confidence, and hunger for the future filled me. I looked eagerly around the Pullman car.

In 1957, the South was rigorously segregated, but sitting across from me was a beautiful black woman whose traveling suit was more elegant than my own. I knew little of the political and economic realities of the South. Although I had never known a black person who was not a servant, a black person was really the same as a white person to me. The black people I had known had always been loving and encouraging toward me. It seemed rather strange that this woman should be sharing my Pullman seat, but the situation didn't unsettle me—I had inherited my mother's openness to people.

We began to talk. Her name was Anabel, her father was a doctor in Atlanta, and she was going to Howard University in Washington. She would be a freshman. She said that she wanted to study history but that she loved to cook so much she would miss her mother's kitchen. I told her that I too loved to cook.

"There are so few good restaurants in the South. Only in private homes—"

"Yes," said Anabel, "my mother really knows how to cook for company."

I asked her to have lunch with me in the dining car. I knew that blacks were not welcome in dining cars, but I was struck with the injustice of Anabel's situation. Would she be forced to consume a peanut butter sandwich out of a paper bag while everyone else on the train dined on filet mignon and cherries jubilee? In asking her to have lunch with me I didn't consciously intend to act courageously—it just seemed the natural, human thing to do.

Anabel said she would be happy to join me for lunch. She seemed nervous. Suddenly, I was nervous too, thinking about what we were going to do. We walked toward the dining car, trying to keep our balance on the unreliably swaying train—one moment the smoothness of the movement filled me with overconfidence, the next moment I was jerked and shaken and nearly thrown off my feet. Anabel and I were met at the entrance to the dining car by the steward. I smiled at him. "Is there a table for two available?"

He looked at me. His eyes passed from my face to Anabel's, his surprise gradually turning into anger.

"Could we be seated by the window, please?" I said. "We're going through beautiful country. But it won't be fall for a long time, will it?"

The steward looked confused. "Yes, miss," he said. "Fall is a long way off." He brushed off the sleeves of his crisp blue suit, straightened his tie. "I'll see what's available, miss."

He turned and walked briskly down the aisle, glancing left and right. Anabel and I could see that there were several seats available. By this time the other passengers had begun to notice us. Some of them craned their necks around to look. The steward returned from the far end of the car, his face full of confusion and indecision.

"There is a place for one available, miss," he said. All conversation at the tables had stopped. The train was passing over a long, smooth stretch of track, so there was not much outside noise to distract us. I clutched my purse tightly so no one could see that my hands were trembling. I felt my knees were going to give way.

"I'll wait until there is a table for two available," I said, "so that I can have lunch with my friend." Although I knew I was speaking softly, my voice sounded very loud to me.

"Very well," said the steward. He turned around quickly and busied himself pouring coffee from the silver pot at a nearby table.

I looked at Anabel. She was standing very straight and tall and she looked even more beautiful than she had in the Pullman car. I knew my face was tense and grim, my smile forced and awkward, my movements clumsy—I always felt myself become ugly under pressure.

We waited only about five minutes, but it seemed an hour. The steward poured more coffee into the already full cups, asked the people at the table what they wanted for dessert, and told the white-coated waiter to brush the bread crumbs off the starched tablecloth. Then he turned abruptly to me and said, "I have a table for two now, miss."

Anabel and I followed him down the aisle. Everyone in the dining car was aware of us, but no one turned and stared, and there were no comments. When we reached our table, the steward pulled out my chair and seated me. Anabel was still standing. He hesitated. Would he seat Anabel or wouldn't he? I looked her in the eyes and tried to send her a message: "Don't seat yourself. Wait for him to do it." Fear and indecision flickered across her face. She seemed to falter, then recover herself. She remained standing.

"What a beautiful view you've given us," I said. "Right by the window."

The steward's face turned red, he mumbled something, and then he pulled out Anabel's chair. She slipped into her seat, laid her purse and gloves on the table, smiled at him, and said, "Thank you." He handed us menus, turned, and almost ran down the aisle toward the kitchen. I held the open menu in front of my face. I was afraid to look at Anabel. It was several minutes before I realized that my menu was upside-down.

Outside the window, the lush green Southern landscape stretched out indolently beneath the hot September sun: burgeoning forests, fields where the corn was dense and high, meandering brown-green rivers. We talked, no longer frightened and tense, with the openness and optimism natural to both of us. Everything seemed propitious to encourage our friendship. We were enclosed by the moving train and our recent success in a kind of enchanted bubble that freed us from normal reticence.

I told her about my great-grandfather, Edward Copeland, a businessman who was good to his employees. If a woman who worked at his mill became pregnant, he paid for good medical care. He tried to help.

"My father was like him," I said, "but he died young."

Anabel explained that her grandfather had grown up on a plantation in Alabama. She looked out the window at the paradisical Southern land. "The owner beat him," she said softly. He had lived in a house that was in such bad condition the rain fell on his face when he was in bed at night. He told her how he planted corn. He would dig a hole in the earth, put in four seeds, make a little mountain of dirt over them, then say, "One for the cutworm, one for the crow, one for God, and one to grow."

"I guess I was the seed that grew," she said.

I told her that my grandmother had given me Edward Copeland's Bible and that written on the flyleaf were two words: "Honor everyone." Anabel lowered her head. There were tears in her eyes.

No longer hostile and uneasy, everyone in the dining car seemed to be enjoying the good food, the sunlight flickering across the tables, the rhythm of the train's movement. I no longer felt that I was a brazen pariah for what I had done. Southerners are brought up to be strongly respectful, almost fearful, of authority. To act contrary to the laws of ancestors, of fathers, was something I found very hard to do. But I hadn't actually defied authority; I had more or less gotten around it. I had simply smiled our way into the whites-only dining car. "You catch more flies with honey than with vinegar," Henretta would say.

The next morning the train arrived in Washington. Anabel gathered together her luggage.

"I never expected to find a friend on this train," she said. As we stood facing each other in the aisle, she reached out and touched me lightly on the arm.

I felt weak, almost faint. I didn't know if I was equal to this greatness. But Anabel was. She stood on the station platform, waving good-bye to me, her back straight, her arms strong, until the train pulled away. I never saw her again, but she is always with me. Sometimes I imagine that I have invited her to dinner and I plan a menu worthy of her grace and courage.

Menu IX:

This is for Anabel.

Georgia Creamed Chicken

Zucchini with Nutmeg

Fresh Corn Spoon Bread

Marie's Chocolate Cake
with Bourbon, Almonds, and Raisins

Georgia Creamed Chicken

$\mathcal{A}$ great dish for company that can be made ahead.

> 2 chickens, cut up, together weighing 5 pounds
> 6 cups chicken stock
> 1 cup sherry
> 2 tablespoons butter
> 2 tablespoons flour
> 1¼ cups light cream (half and half)
> 2 tablespoons chopped fresh parsley
> ⅛ teaspoon white pepper
> 1 teaspoon grated onion
> ½ pound mushrooms, sliced, sautéed in
>   2 tablespoons butter
> salt
> 2 cups fresh bread crumbs
> small bits of butter

1. Cook the chicken in stock until tender, about 40 minutes. Cool and remove meat from bones; cut into small pieces. Place the chicken in a bowl and cover with sherry. Let marinate for 1 hour, turning chicken frequently. Drain off sherry.

2. Melt butter in a large skillet, add flour, and cook roux for 2 minutes over low heat. Remove from heat and slowly add cream, stirring constantly. Add the parsley, pepper, and grated onion. Cook, stirring until sauce thickens.

3. Prepare mushrooms and add salt to taste. Add the mushrooms and the chicken to the sauce, and correct the seasoning. Let mixture cool, then chill it.

4. Pour chilled mixture into a large, buttered ovenproof casserole, sprinkle with bread crumbs and dot with bits of butter.

5. Bake in a 350°F oven for about 35 minutes, or until chicken is hot and crumbs are browned. Serve with rice.

8 servings

Zucchini with Nutmeg

Somehow, the nutmeg offsets the zucchini in just the right way.

3 pounds zucchini
1 teaspoon nutmeg
salt
pepper
3 tablespoons butter
3 tablespoons sour cream or ½ cup heavy cream

1. Cut the zucchini in rounds (do not peel).

2. Bring ¾ cup water to boil in a large skillet. Add the zucchini, lower heat, and cover. Simmer, stirring occasionally, until zucchini is tender and water has evaporated.

3. Crush the zucchini with a wooden spoon. Add the nutmeg, salt, pepper, butter, and cream. Serve hot.

8 servings

Fresh Corn Spoon Bread

A classic Southern dish.

4–5 ears tender young corn	1½ teaspoons sugar
4 cups milk, divided	3 eggs, separated
1 cup white corn meal	¼ teaspoon grated nutmeg
1 teaspoon salt	¼ teaspoon white pepper
1 stick butter	

1. Preheat oven to 325°F.

2. With a small sharp knife, cut down the middle of each row of kernels of the corn, making long slices down the cob. Cut the kernels from the cob into a bowl, then scrape the pulp from the cobs into the bowl until you have 2 cups of corn and pulp.

3. Pour 2 cups of the milk into a large saucepan and bring to boil over medium heat (be careful not to burn the milk). Add the corn and let the mixture come back to a boil. Add the corn meal and the salt, and stir constantly until mixture begins to thicken.

4. Remove from heat. Add the butter and sugar, and beat well. Stir in the remaining 2 cups milk and beat well.

5. Beat the egg yolks and add to the mixture. Add the white pepper and the nutmeg.

6. Beat the egg whites until stiff. Fold delicately into cornmeal mixture.

7. Butter a large casserole or soufflé dish and pour in mixture. Bake for about 1 hour. When done, bread should be puffed and browned, like a soufflé. Serve immediately with butter.

8 servings

Marie's Chocolate Cake with Bourbon, Almonds, and Raisins

*A*lso a nice cake to serve at Christmas time.

> ½ cup bourbon whiskey
> 1 cup golden seedless raisins
> 1 pound semisweet chocolate
> 2 sticks unsalted butter
> 1¼ cups sugar
> 6 eggs, separated
> 2 cups cake flour
> 1¼ pounds (20 ounces) ground almonds
>   (may be ground in blender or food processor,
>   small amounts at a time, at top speed for 30 seconds)
> pinch of salt

For the Icing:

> 1 stick unsalted butter
> 4 ounces semisweet chocolate

1. Combine the whiskey and the raisins and let soak for at least 2 hours.

2. Preheat oven to 300°F.

3. In a small saucepan, melt semisweet chocolate and 1 stick of the butter over *very* low heat; stir until smooth and creamy.

4. In a large bowl, cream with an electric mixer the remaining 1 stick butter and 1¼ cups sugar. Add 6 egg yolks, beating well; add flour gradually, beating well. Add melted chocolate and whiskey and raisins.

5. Now put aside electric mixer and use a spatula. Incorporate almonds into cake mixture. Batter will be very stiff.

6. Whip egg whites with a pinch of salt until stiff; blend ¼ of the egg whites into cake mixture; then blend carefully ⅓ of remaining whites. Repeat until all egg whites are incorporated.

7. Generously butter a 12-inch mold or large tube pan. Pour batter into pan and bake in oven for 40 minutes. The cake should be soft in the center. Cool 1 hour before unmolding.

8. To make the icing, stir butter and chocolate in a medium saucepan over *very* low heat until smooth and creamy. Take pan from heat and cool until mixture is of icing consistency.

9. Spread cake with icing, covering top and sides. Keep cake covered until ready to serve. Do not freeze.

16 servings (1 cup of icing)

Luann at Radcliffe

A Green
Silk Dress

AT THE END of my first semester at college, I spent Christmas in Greensboro with Judge and Miss Lady. After living in the Northeast, I was struck with the security, self-sufficiency, and indolence of the Greensboro world. I became aware of the sound of my family's voices; my Georgia relatives spoke slowly, softly, with a musical cadence that rose and fell rhythmically. They seemed to have native expressions for everything that happened in their lives, everything they wanted to talk about. The language, the food, the interiors, the landscape of this world fit together—all seemed sensuous and sweet.

But even though there was comfort in being at home, I was uneasy. When I left for college, Judge had given me a check to cover my book expenses, but I had spent all of it on clothes. I had had every intention of buying the books I needed and wanted, but when a friend from school took me to Bonwit Teller in downtown Boston, I was so entranced with this beautiful place and its elegant merchandise that I forgot all about the Pelican edition of Shakespeare. The store was filled with contemporary versions of Aunt Clare's clothes and the kinds of things Miss Lady had brought back from Europe. I bought a green silk dinner dress and several other exquisite, unnecessary items.

Miss Lady was upset and Judge was exasperated and angry. What I had done confirmed what he had known all along—I was encountering bad influences in the North. He let me know that there would be no more book money forthcoming. Now I was afraid that Judge and Miss Lady would convince my mother that I must not go back to college, and the house was filled with tension. I thought of the lovely clothes I had bought, and they no longer gave me pleasure. I realized that I would have to live without the books that were so important to me, books that would teach me how to live and how to write.

I wanted to make a contribution to Christmas dinner as my Christmas gift to Judge and Miss Lady. I asked Miss Lady to let me help. She doubted that my cooking would ever measure up to her standards; only Henretta could do things right for Miss Lady. But finally she said that I could make the dessert, with Henretta's help.

On Christmas Eve morning I woke up happy and impatient to make a Tennessee jam cake. Today would be filled with work I loved. I could hear Judge and LeRoy downstairs setting up the Christmas tree in the bay window of the living room, untangling the ropes of bells they would hang on the branches. The smell of freshly cut evergreens drifted up the stairs. In the fireplaces of every room in the house burned the wood fires that Henretta laid every morning at dawn.

I stopped in to see Miss Lady, as I always did in the morning, when she was having breakfast in bed. Propped up on the pillows in her pink silk bed jacket, the tray balanced on her knees, gesturing delicately with the silver fork at the scrambled eggs, her face soft and unassembled, Miss Lady seemed to say that if she could just get through breakfast she would be equal to the coming day. I stood by the side of her bed and she gave me her hand. "Did you sleep well, darling?" she asked. Her hands felt like little birds that had fallen out of their tree, still warm, still throbbing; I could feel the delicate bones beneath the skin that was soft as down.

She picked up a piece of toast and nibbled at it. Henretta always cut the crusts off the loaf bread ("light bread," she called it) before she buttered and toasted it. Bread with the crusts left on was considered common. Miss Lady examined the piece of toast, then laid it lightly down on the plate. It met with her approval. In a few minutes she would confer with Henretta about the most important thing in the world, this day that was about to begin in this house in Greensboro, Georgia.

Like sisters, Miss Lady and Henretta loved each other and were jealous of each other. Sometimes they were delicate, so as not to hurt each other's feelings. Other times they said blunt things, then cried, agonized, and made up. Psychologically they were equals. Miss Lady fretted and fussed at Henretta, but she knew who Henretta was. Even though she had grown up on a dirt farm, Henretta was a great chef, a genius who could not read or write. Miss Lady knew this and appreciated it, although she would not have used the word *genius*. And as someone who had lived with Miss Lady throughout her adult life, Henretta understood Miss Lady and her delicate nerves. Miss Lady *must* have freshly ironed embroidered linen on her breakfast tray, the biscuits must be very small and very light, the chicken salad must be made from white meat, the peaches for peach ice cream must be very ripe, the rose in the bud vase in the guest room must be perfectly red and budding. "Everything," Henretta explained, "must be just right for Miss Lady, because Miss Lady was raised tenderly and that's what she's used to."

Henretta's kitchen, a big, light-filled room, was warmed by the fire that roared in the wood stove. Every morning at dawn she got the fire going—she knew how to control the temperature by starting with newspaper and kindling, adding logs, and maneuvering the embers with the poker. Some things were cooked on the wood stove, some on the electric, and only Henretta understood the distinction between them. She had laid out the ingredients for my cake on the kitchen table along with the pottery mixing bowls.

I was a little nervous about being responsible for the dessert for Miss Lady's Christmas dinner, but I never really doubted that my cake would turn out. Even when I was seventeen, cooking was something I did with confidence. I had spent so many hours sitting at the kitchen table, watching Henretta— learning to fold in the egg whites a little at a time to lighten the batter, to add the olive oil to the egg yolks in tiny droplets so the mayonnaise wouldn't turn, to arrange the cucumber sandwiches on the platter and put the parsley garnish in just the right places. Henretta let me taste and try, and she taught me her secrets. She worked by instinct, never opening a cookbook. Even as a young girl, I worried that Henretta's cooking would be lost, that she would grow old and there would be no record of her life's work, that it would live only in the memory of a few people whose imaginations were not equal to hers.

Henretta imparted to me not only her art but her confidence. I discovered that if I used fresh ingredients and if I performed each step of the recipe in good order, in good time, I would achieve a successful result. I always had the wonderful sense of things happening as they *should* happen, of steady effort leading to tangible results. Creaming the butter and sugar, adding the preserves and the fragrant spices, folding in the egg whites lightly and firmly—while my hands performed this pleasurable work, my mind played in a kind of reverie. My past made sense, my present was full, my future would be happy.

Soon the batter in the bowl was shiny and thick. I licked the wooden spoon. "You won't have any cake left, Miss Luann, if you keep tasting," Henretta warned. I poured the cake into two large, round cake pans, and Henretta put them into the electric oven.

Henretta kept up a running dialogue. Ostensibly she was talking to me, but she was also talking to herself, exploring, elaborating, justifying her experience and her life. She insisted that I was just like Miss Lady and my father, and Susan was just like Judge. This pleased her enormously; she took full credit for the family's continuity in breeding and elegance. All her anger and vituperation were reserved for what she called "trash," people who were not ladies and gentlemen. It would be terrible if any of us in her family should associate with trash or—the worst thing that could happen—marry trash.

Henretta considered herself responsible for building the characters of the young people in the family and for holding backsliding adults to high standards. As important as taste was to Henretta, it was secondary to personal integrity. Miss Lady seemed to assume that being born into a good family assured one's being a lady or a gentleman, but Henretta and Judge looked beneath the surface trappings to the underlying character.

Henretta insisted that things be done in the traditional way. She was the watchful guardian of all the treasure contained in Miss Lady's house, which would be duly apportioned out to the rightful heirs. Lovingly she cared for the Eli Terry clock that would "go to Miss Susan," the Vieux Paris vases that would "go to Miss Luann," the silver tea and coffee service that would "go to Miss Virginia." A chip or a dent in these precious things would be disastrous, just as any illegitimacy, any misalliance, any breach of etiquette or decorum threatened the stability of the family and the divinely established order of the world.

Telling her long cautionary tales about the dreadful events that would happen in our family and Greensboro "if ladies and gentlemen got mixed up with trash," Henretta always ended with an affirmation of her faith: no matter how bad the situation looked, Judge, Mr. Copeland, or God would set things straight, as if the three of them were permanently installed on golden thrones that hung suspended in the sky over Greensboro.

"Working with hot sugar is mighty risky," Henretta said, as I cooked the icing. I added milk, cream, butter, and vanilla to the caramelized sugar, beat for a long time, until the icing held its shape, dipped my finger in, and tasted.

Henretta took the cakes out of the oven and set them on a shelf in the pantry to cool. As I put away the mixing bowls, I regarded my handiwork: two beautiful golden cakes. Were they rich, but light too? Had I added just the right amount of cinnamon? I scooped a small piece from the center of one of the cakes. Delicious! I took another piece. Wonderful! I looked around and saw that Henretta was working at the sink, her back turned to the pantry.

Soon I had eaten a hole in the center of the cake. I fell further into torment with each bite I took. I had summoned discipline, self-control to make the cake. I had balanced myself on that plateau. Now I was sliding down the mountain of self-indulgence, unable to stop myself.

There were holes now in the center of both cakes. Henretta opened the pantry door.

"What are you doing in here, Miss Luann?"

"Look at those cakes!" she exclaimed. "You've eaten holes in Miss Lady's jam cake!"

"I'm sorry," I stammered.

"The Lord preserve us. What will Miss Lady say?"

I burst into tears. Henretta put her arms around me, stroked my hair. "Now don't you worry, Miss Luann. We'll just fill those holes with icing. Miss Lady will never know the difference."

Henretta and I iced the cake and filled the holes with icing. As a finishing touch, she dipped a knife in hot water and ran it over the surface, smoothing and polishing. The cake looked like perfection.

AT ONE O'CLOCK on Christmas day, we seated ourselves at the dinner table. Miss Lady and Judge expected the best, as usual, and they were not disappointed in the Christmas turkey, brown and buttery, with the dressing over which Henretta had labored for two days, the hot yeast rolls, the rich sweet potatoes.

On this day, as on every other day in Greensboro, the smells from the kitchen filled Miss Lady's house with the sense of expectancy, the premonition that something good was going to happen, that always preceded midday dinner.

But even the prospect of good food had not relieved the tension at the dinner table. Judge was not only angry but perplexed. He did not understand a young woman who had wanted to be a writer all her life (a dubious profession, in his opinion) and then, given the chance to become one, had spent her book money on a silk dress. I was too confused to defend myself, as bewildered by my impulsiveness and irrationality as Judge was. Miss Lady, hypersensitive as always to Judge's moods, was on the verge of tears.

"Tell us a story, Judge," she said, blotting her eyes with her handkerchief.

Judge immediately looked more cheerful. Telling a story was the best thing he could do. But he was in a difficult position—he had to say something that would amuse Miss Lady and that would also enlighten me about the true and proven way to live.

He leaned back in his chair and balanced his cigarette on the ashtray beside his plate. "Last year I made a special trip to Atlanta. I had decided to give Miss Lady a book. She is a lady who reads. Has all sorts of things going on in her head I have no notion of. I thought she would appreciate a book, if I could find the right one, to let her know I remembered her birthday. Well, I called up one of my poker friends and asked him the name of the bookstore in Atlanta he favored. Cooper's was his choice. So I took myself off to Cooper's. No sooner had I walked in than I felt befuddled. What a bewildering array of the printed word! I spied a table with a sign saying, 'Books by William Faulkner.' That name rang a bell. I had heard that name somewhere before. I asked the saleslady if he was a reputable author. 'He is one of our most famous,' she said. Right underneath my hand was a book entitled *Requiem for a Nun*. What a beautiful title for a religious book, I thought. I had the saleslady wrap it up on the spot."

Judge paused. "So I presented *Requiem for a Nun* to Miss Lady on her birthday." He paused again. "That book is not about nuns. Doesn't have a thing in the world to do with nuns. Not fit for a lady's eyes!"

He continued. "How could I make it up to Miss Lady? How could I get back in her good graces? I thought of a dealer in rare books that I knew of in New York City. Mr. Copeland ordered things from him. Of course I realized that he might have gone out of business. But I decided to take a chance. I wrote him a letter. Told him that I was a man of a certain age who didn't hold with the newfangled literature. That I wanted a book to give to my wife on her birthday. That my wife was a mighty sweet woman. Lo and behold, the fellow answered me. And sent a *beautiful* book. I think I can say with certainty that Miss Lady was pleased. Elizabeth Barrett Browning's *Sonnets from the Portuguese*. Now, that's what I call a book!"

I had seen it lying on Miss Lady's bedside table, next to her Bible. It was small, bound in soft red leather, embossed with gold lilies, and the pages were thin, pearly, crisp, edged in gold leaf. One would have to read this book very carefully, so as not to offend it. I thought of my school books, how I marked them up, carried them around in my purse, dropped them on the floor, sometimes woke up to find them under my pillow.

I thought of my friends at college. What would they think of my grandfather, a man who didn't know who Faulkner was? I was afraid that Judge and Miss Lady would decide that the intellectually sophisticated world of Harvard that I found so exciting was too radical and dangerous for a girl who had had such a sheltered upbringing.

It seemed that Henretta would take forever clearing the table for dessert. Finally she brought in the cake, set it down before me, and handed me a cake knife. She stood beside Miss Lady's chair, and we didn't dare look at each other. Miss Lady tilted her head to one side, tasted her serving of cake, and laid her fork down on her plate. She arched her hand a little, the way she always did when she was tasting and considering.

"Darling," she said, "this is the best jam cake I *ever* tasted." Then she became aware that Henretta was standing at her elbow. "As good as when Henretta makes it!" The cake was sagging in the middle and leaning a little, lopsided, but Judge and Miss Lady had not noticed.

"It's a mighty fine cake, honey," said Judge. There was a delighted smile on his face, and his blue eyes were sparkling. Although his granddaughter was a student at Harvard, she was really just like his mother, Miss Della. She could make the Tennessee jam cake. I knew that I would be returning to college for the spring semester.

Menu x:

The meal that saved my college education.

Chilled Salmon Mousse

Roast Turkey with Pecan Dressing

Sweet Potatoes with
Bourbon Sauce

Creamed Spinach and Artichokes

Cousin Catherine's Potato Yeast Rolls

Tennessee Jam Cake with
Caramel Icing

Chilled Salmon Mousse

A terrific appetizer for any party.

> 2 envelopes gelatin
> ½ cup cold water
> 1 cup boiling water
> 2 tablespoons lemon juice
> 2 tablespoons white wine vinegar
> ½ teaspoon salt
> 1 cup mayonnaise (homemade, see page 83,
>   Chilled Sweetbreads Salad)
> 1 cup heavy cream, whipped
> 3 tablespoons Worcestershire sauce
> 1 small onion, grated
> 2 cups red salmon, flaked
> 1 large cucumber, peeled, seeded, finely chopped
> 1 teaspoon fresh minced dill
> watercress for garnish

1. In a medium bowl, soften the gelatin in cold water. Add boiling water and stir until gelatin dissolves. Add the lemon juice, vinegar, and salt. Cool in the refrigerator about one hour.

2. In a large bowl, mix the mayonnaise and the whipped cream. Add the cooled gelatin mixture. Stir in the Worcestershire sauce, onion, salmon, chopped cucumber, and dill.

3. Oil a fish mold or a 10-inch round mold, and pour in the salmon mixture. Cover and put in refrigerator to congeal, about 4 hours.

4. Plunge mold for a few seconds into a basin of hot water coming just up to the sides. Unmold on platter and surround with watercress.

12 servings

Roast Turkey with Pecan Dressing

The pecan dressing really makes this stand out from the usual Thanksgiving fare.

    1 16–18 pound turkey
    the liver from the turkey
    11 tablespoons unsalted butter, divided
    2 cups salted pecans, chopped
    16 slices white bread (homemade type)
    4 tablespoons lard
    1 teaspoon salt
    1 teaspoon black pepper
    1 teaspoon celery seed, crushed
    1 teaspoon thyme
    1 tablespoon finely chopped fresh parsley
    ½ nutmeg, grated
    ½ cup boiling water
    6 hard-boiled eggs
    ¼ teaspoon ground mace
    10 large mushrooms, finely chopped
    ½ cup sherry
    1 large onion, grated

1. Cook the turkey liver the day before you make the dressing: simmer it for 30 minutes in lightly salted water, then drain and store in refrigerator until ready to use.

2. Melt 4 tablespoons of the butter in a medium saucepan. Add the chopped pecans. Transfer to baking sheet, spread out well, and toast in 350°F oven for 5 to 10 minutes, being careful not to burn them. When

brown, remove pecans from oven, and salt them in the pan. Remove from pan and drain on paper towels. Set aside.

3. To make the dressing, toast the white bread until it is dry and crisp. Cool, then powder it with a rolling pin. Transfer crumbs to a large bowl, and add 3 tablespoons of the lard, 4 tablespoons of the butter, salt, black pepper, crushed celery seed, thyme, parsley, and grated nutmeg. Pour in the boiling water and mix thoroughly.

4. Separate the whites from the yolks of the hard-boiled eggs. Rice the whites and add to the mixture. Rub the yolks with the mace and add to the mixture. Add the salted pecans, mushrooms, and sherry. Mix well.

5. Melt the remaining 1 tablespoon lard in a skillet over medium-high heat, and add grated onion. Pound and powder the turkey liver and add to onion and lard; fry until brown. Allow liver mixture to cool, then add to dressing.

6. Stuff turkey cavity and secure legs. (Place remaining dressing in a casserole and, just before serving, bake at 350°F for 30 minutes.) Preheat oven to 450°F. Rub turkey all over with salt and pepper and the remaining 3 tablespoons unsalted butter. Place turkey in roasting pan, put in oven, lower heat to 350°F, and bake, basting frequently with pan juices, until meat thermometer registers 190°F, about 25 minutes per pound.

7. When turkey is done, degrease pan juices, correct the seasoning, and heat to make a sauce. Serve turkey on large platter garnished with parsley, with the sauce in sauceboat. Accompany with baked pecan dressing.

Serves 12 to 15

Sweet Potatoes with Bourbon Sauce

*E*veryone has their version of sweet potatoes, but I wouldn't think of having them without bourbon sauce.

> 6 large sweet potatoes, cooked, mashed
> 1 stick butter
> 1 tablespoon flour
> ¾ cup heavy cream
> 2¾ cups sugar
> 2 eggs, well beaten
> ⅓ cup bourbon whiskey
> 1 teaspoon vanilla
> 1½ cups black walnuts, chopped

1. In a large bowl, blend mashed sweet potatoes with ½ stick butter and whip until light, adding a little cream if necessary. Set aside.

2. In a medium saucepan, melt ½ stick of the butter. Add flour and cook roux 2 minutes. Add cream, 2 cups of the sugar, and eggs. Set aside.

3. Caramelize the remaining ¾ cup sugar: add 3 tablespoons water to sugar in a heavy saucepan, then boil over medium-high heat for 5 to 7 minutes, stirring with a wooden spoon, until sugar is nut brown. Add to sauce. Bring sauce to simmer and cook 2 to 3 minutes until caramelized sugar is melted into sauce. Add bourbon whiskey and beat until thick. Add vanilla.

4. Heap potatoes in a fluffy mound on platter; pour sauce over; sprinkle with walnuts, or add walnuts to sauce and serve separately.

8 servings

Creamed Spinach and Artichokes

This is adapted from one of Aunt Virginia's Georgia cookbooks. You may double the recipe for a buffet. When I served this dish in France, my friends loved it.

> 2 packages frozen chopped spinach
> 1 stick butter
> 8 ounces cream cheese
> salt
> pepper
> juice of ½ lemon
> 2 cans artichoke hearts, drained
> 1 cup fresh bread crumbs
> little bits of butter

1. Preheat oven to 350°F.

2. Cook the spinach, drain, and set aside.

3. In a large saucepan, melt the butter and cream cheese over low heat.

4. Add the drained spinach, salt, pepper, and lemon juice. Mix well. Cut artichoke hearts into small pieces and arrange in the bottom of a 9-by-12-inch ovenproof dish. Pour the spinach mixture over.

5. Sprinkle with bread crumbs and dot with bits of butter.

6. Bake in oven for 30 minutes.

6 servings

Cousin Catherine's Potato Yeast Rolls

*L*ight and tasty. This recipe may be halved.

> 1⅓ envelopes yeast
> ½ cup lukewarm water
> ⅔ cup butter, melted
> ½ cup sugar
> 2 teaspoons salt
> 1 cup mashed potatoes
> 1 cup scalded milk (milk heated to
>   just below boiling point)
> 2 eggs, well beaten
> about 8 cups flour

1. In a small bowl, dissolve yeast in warm water (105°–115°F).
2. In a large mixing bowl, blend together butter, sugar, salt, mashed potatoes, and scalded milk. When cool, add yeast; mix well. Add beaten eggs. Stir in enough flour to make stiff dough.
3. Put dough in greased bowl large enough to allow slight rising. Cover bowl tightly with damp cloth, and put in refrigerator until ready to roll out.
4. Two or three hours before baking time, sprinkle an ample amount of flour on a pastry board, and knead the dough until smooth and elastic, about 1 to 2 minutes.
5. Roll out dough about ¾ inch thick and cut into circles with a 3-inch cutter or a wide glass. Fold round shapes in half and pinch together; put them a small distance apart on greased baking pans.
6. Let rise uncovered in a warm place until ready to bake (2 to 3 hours). You may set them in a *barely* warm oven, uncovered, to rise. Bake in a preheated 375°F oven until brown, about 10–15 minutes. Serve hot with butter.

5 dozen rolls

Tennessee Jam Cake with Caramel Icing

This cake is better if made two or three days in advance and allowed to mellow. The jams add a moist texture to the cake.

1 tablespoon lemon juice

1 cup milk

2 sticks butter

1 cup sugar

1 cup blackberry jam

1 cup strawberry preserves

1 cup fig preserves

5 eggs, separated

1 tablespoon baking soda

3 cups flour

1 tablespoon cinnamon

1 tablespoon allspice

1 cup pecans, finely ground

For the Caramel Icing:

1½ cups milk

5 cups sugar, separated

4 tablespoons butter, separated

1 cup light cream (half and half)

2 teaspoons vanilla

1. Preheat oven to 325°F. Butter and flour three 9-inch round cake pans.

2. Add 1 tablespoon lemon juice to 1 cup milk and allow to stand at least 10 minutes.

3. In a large bowl, cream butter and sugar; add jam and preserves, and mix well. Add egg yolks and beat well.

4. In separate bowl, add soda to flour. Add flour alternately with sour milk to jam mixture, and mix well after each addition. Add the spices and the ground pecans, and mix well. Beat the egg whites until stiff and fold delicately into cake mixture.

5. Pour batter into cake pans and bake in oven for 50 minutes, or until toothpick inserted in center comes out clean. Frost with caramel icing.

6. To make the icing, combine milk and 4 cups of the sugar in a large saucepan over low heat. Do not boil.

7. Caramelize the remaining 1 cup sugar: add 4 tablespoons water to sugar in a heavy saucepan. Bring to boil over medium-high heat. Stir with a wooden spoon until sugar is nut brown. This will take 5 to 7 minutes. Pour caramelized sugar into mixture of hot milk and sugar. Add 2 tablespoons of the butter and the cream. Cook and stir over medium-high heat until sugar melts and mixture comes to soft-ball stage (240°F on candy thermometer).

8. Remove from heat, add the remaining 2 tablespoons butter and the vanilla. Cool to room temperature, then beat until thick enough to spread on cake. If icing gets too stiff, add a little cream.

12 servings

Henretta with Susan and Luann

Sisters

$\mathcal{W}$HEN I WAS nine and Susan was seven and we were living
in Nashville during the school year, we were assigned a chore: on alternate
days we were to empty the garbage pail into the can in the alley behind the
house. We always had to be reminded.

One day Susan went out the back door with the pail in hand, was gone for
a long time, and finally returned without the pail but carrying an ancient, pink
plush, moth-eaten pincushion with "Welcome to Niagara" spelled out in rusty
metallic thread. This became Susan's favorite possession; she kept it in her
room and liked it much better than the neatly elegant dolls Miss Lady had
given her. (Many years later, when Susan was studying at the Pennsylvania
Academy of Fine Arts, the pincushion, her "found object," was the focal point
of her collage that won first prize in the school competition.)

On one of the days when it was my turn to empty the garbage, I too was gone for a very long time, and I returned to the house (also without the pail, which was long forgotten) smelling a blue morning glory. I looked for a vase small enough to hold it and finally found one of Murlo's antique crystal liqueur glasses that she kept on the dining-room sideboard beside her bottle of anisette. I washed and polished it and worked for a long time trying to make the ephemeral and soon-to-be-drooping morning glory curve gracefully out of the glass. I set it on the windowsill in Murlo's room and for a few moments, with the sunlight shining through the crystal and the translucent blue petals, it was serenely perfect.

Then the wind moved the curtain; a moment later the glass lay in pieces on the floor. Suddenly, Murlo was standing in the doorway. "What have you done?" she demanded. Her anger so scared me that when I tried to find words of explanation, I began to cry. My mother entered just then, understood what had happened, and to Murlo's repeated question, "Why did she break my glass?" my mother said, "She was trying to make something beautiful." "Yes," I sobbed, "yes," relief flooding through me. Murlo relented, willing as always to encourage high ambitions.

That afternoon, knowing I was in favor, I took a pound of sugar from the pantry, poured it on the dining-room table, and began to make "snow mountains." Dazzling mounds rose and collapsed beneath my hands. Murlo and my mother passed through the room occasionally, looking somewhat bewildered, but there was a slight smile on Murlo's face. "Yes," she seemed to be saying to herself, "that child is trying to create Beauty."

But it was Susan who always knew how to please Murlo. They genuinely loved each other's company. They read and sewed together, singing the "Whif-fenpoof Song" and "When You Come to the End of a Perfect Day." I could tell that Murlo always approved of Susan's projects, even if she did not actually voice her praise of them. But no matter how hard I practiced the first movement of the *Moonlight Sonata*, my playing never seemed to come up to Murlo's standards.

I sensed Murlo's private conviction that she and Susan (and Judge) possessed the only true "blue blood" in the family, as people with backbone and good character, whereas Miss Lady and I had soft and selfish constitutions. And my mother was too easygoing and irresponsible.

Wanting to join in Murlo and Susan's charmed circle, I drew a picture of a cow, its head a portrait of Murlo, and gave it a name: "Moolo." Laughing, I showed my hilarious illustration to Murlo. She adjusted her glasses and looked at it closely.

"This is very vulgar," she said.

Crushed, I took the drawing and tore it up. That word *vulgar* assumed large proportions and rang in my head for a long time.

E very summer when my family arrived at Miss Lady and Judge's house in Greensboro, Susan and I would dart in the house to change out of our city clothes and into our blue jeans, and we'd take off our shoes. Susan ran all over the yard, but I was tenderfooted and went barefoot only in the house. I was enchanted by the grand piano in the parlor and spent many hours practicing (much to Miss Lady's delight and Judge's consternation). I gathered flowers from the garden and arranged them in Miss Lady's everyday vases, which she kept on the back porch, while Susan swung from the branches of the crabapple tree.

Judge loved to take us fishing (or thought he did) and would ceremoniously assemble the bamboo poles, the picnic lunch, and the life jackets. This was Susan's chance to show everyone that she was better at roughing it than I was. But once she was in the rowboat, beset by heat and mosquitoes and so excited she needed to pee-pee every five minutes, she proved herself hardly more of a trooper than I was. We couldn't bear to see Judge bait the hooks with earthworms—our screams frightened away the fish, he said—and if Susan caught a fish, she leaped to her feet, jumped up and down, leaned way overboard to bring the fish in, and very nearly capsized the boat. The fastidious femininity that Judge found so charming in the parlor and on the front porch was a "damn nuisance" on a fishing trip. When Judge asked Susan why she couldn't behave herself on a fishing trip, Susan replied that she "felt sorry for the earthworms." Judge shook his head. "She feels sorry for the earthworms!" he muttered.

But there was rarely any strain on the bond between Judge and Susan. She was Judge's child and I was Miss Lady's. Susan noticed many things that proved Miss Lady favored me (unlike Murlo, who was supposedly noble and impartial). As my magnolia grew and flourished in the side yard, Susan complained that there had been no tree planted for *her*. Miss Lady said, "I planted the magnolia tree in the side yard when Luann was born and have always called it her tree. The live oak in the backyard is Jimmy's tree. Naturally, I do not love my other grandchildren any less but just gave out of places to plant trees." Susan found this explanation neither convincing nor amusing.

Miss Lady and I wanted to create a delicate world in which the kind of beauty we loved could flourish in untroubled serenity. We hated the raw, the ugly, the ungraceful, whereas Susan considered herself a strong, forthright person like Murlo and Judge. Her integrity consisted in looking at reality unflinchingly, without averting her eyes. Miss Lady did not allow us to wear blue jeans when we called on her friends or when we went uptown (one block east of her house). She said, "It's not that I don't like you girls to wear blue jeans, it's just that you look so *sweet* in dresses." Susan, who never wanted to take off her jeans, said that this "wishy-washy diplomacy" offended her even more than a direct command.

WHEN LEROY, THE chaffeur, took Miss Lady for her drive around town after her nap, the itinerary varied little from day to day. Miss Lady seemed never to tire of seeing the same houses and gardens, the courthouse, the bank, the stores uptown, the Episcopal Church, the Presbyterian Church ("more beautiful than our Methodist Church," she always said, "because the architecture is of an earlier date"). She noticed every minute change in the scene: Miss Celeste Smith had pruned her magnolia, Miss Dot's rose garden was almost past its prime, Miss Annie's front porch was newly painted, the McCommons children had a new puppy.

Susan and I usually managed to avoid these excursions, but on one occasion when the drive was scheduled to end with a call on Amy and Theodore Geisler, Miss Lady insisted we go. Brother and sister, Miss Amy and Theodore, as we called them, were our elderly distant cousins. They lived in a rather grand but dilapidated house across the street from the Episcopal

Church. They were supposedly related to the kaiser and had lived in Greensboro for a long time (since the end of World War I, I imagined, when they lost their family estates in Germany and were forced to emigrate). On visits, we would sit in stiff chairs in their musty parlor and look at Theodore's collection of old postcards (mostly brightly colored pictures of birds), his stereopticon, and Miss Amy's antique dolls.

Dressed to Miss Lady's satisfaction in white summer dresses made by Murlo, we finally arrived, after LeRoy had driven us *so* slowly around town, at the Geisler house. We climbed the front porch steps and found Theodore and Miss Amy waiting for us. Theodore held open the screen door. Miss Lady entered, with Susan close behind.

But as Susan stepped across the threshold, Theodore called out "Stop!" in a thunderous voice. Susan froze.

"You are the youngest," Theodore said. "Let Luann enter first. The eldest always goes first." He was a tall man with shaggy white hair. He seemed to tower over Susan threateningly. Susan flinched, then her back stiffened.

"The eldest takes precedence, dear," said tiny Miss Amy.

Susan lifted her chin, and her heels seemed literally to dig into the porch floor.

"That's nonsense," she said. "I won't go in."

"Susan," said Miss Lady gently, "Miss Amy and Theodore are only trying to—that is, trying to show you the manners they learned when they were little."

Susan was silent and did not move.

Miss Lady tried again, "Let's not spoil this nice occasion, dear."

Susan glared at Miss Amy and Theodore and said, "Luann and I will go in together, equal, side by side."

So Susan and I locked arms and passed through the door, shoulder to shoulder, perfectly in step with each other.

ONCE WE WERE teenagers, Susan threw herself into the venture with all the energy and intensity she later gave to raising her son and establishing herself as an artist. Boys poured out their hearts to her. Susan danced to Elvis Presley and I played Chopin. I wasn't as cute as my sister and didn't really want to be, although I envied her for having so many boyfriends when I had so few. Susan was a master of the mores of the world she lived in, while I was a dreamer, always imagining myself as the heroine of the book I was reading or the movie I had seen. When I was eight or nine, I was Jo in *Little Women*. Later, I was Scarlett (and sometimes Melanie). Then Natasha in *War and Peace*, then Elinor in *Sense and Sensibility*. And I tried to dress the parts. I designed an evening dress of blue-green iridescent taffeta and instructed the bewildered dressmaker that the drape around the shoulders be studded with crystal stars. When Susan asked me what inspired the dress, I said, "It's the sky on a clear spring night." I was thinking of Chopin's Nocturne in E-flat, op. 9, no. 2, which I loved to play. Susan, in a strapless dress with tiny waist and a hoop skirt, would have danced the can-can if she could have gotten away with it.

Susan associated the adult world with hypocrisy and constraint, but I was comfortable with people older than myself. They seemed sympathetic to the things I loved—cooking, classical music, and literature. I instinctively trusted grown-ups and believed they were telling me the truth about life. Susan distrusted them, suspecting that they were determined to prevent her from fully enjoying her youth. I wanted to bring people of different generations together, but Susan surrounded herself with teenagers. I wanted people to love one another and be happy and peaceful. Susan liked to bring a situation to a boil.

The summer I was sixteen and Susan fourteen, Miss Lady invited a few of her friends for an afternoon visit, to observe our progress in our music lessons. We would all gather around the piano in the parlor, and Susan and I would be expected to perform.

The white-gloved, soft-voiced ladies took their seats, and Henretta handed around Coca-Cola and iced tea. I must have worn something so discreet I don't remember it (I was in a Melanie mode), but I remember that Susan wore a padded bra, a waist pincher, and a ruff of petticoats under her blouse and skirt. Her bobby socks were held up by rubber bands to just between her ankles and her calves. Her big saddle oxfords protested against the prevailing dainty high-heeled shoes, and (my mother said later) she wore "enough lipstick to paint the side of a barn." I can only describe the look on Miss Lady's face as pained. She suppressed a barely audible sigh and said, "Our Susan is so—*original*."

After a few minutes the ladies grew quiet, and Susan and I understood that the musical moment had arrived.

I played "Träumerei." Away from Murlo's intimidating presence, I relaxed and concentrated on the music. For a few moments, forgetting that I was playing for an audience, I felt in touch with deep emotions. I returned to my seat among the ladies, who were murmuring their approval, whereupon Susan stood up and sang, "I'm Just a Girl Who Can't Say No."

Susan sang well, as she well knew. She sat down, a pleased expression on her face, determined not to break the strained silence, waiting to see how Miss Lady would get out of this one.

Miss Lady rose to her feet, looked straight into the eyes of her friends, smiled, and said, "I believe our Susan is going to have a career in musical comedy."

SUSAN WAS NOT only the most popular girl in Nashville when we were teenagers, she was also one of the best students at the girls' school we attended. She could have gone to any college she chose. She went to Pembroke (now Brown University); she did not want to go to Radcliffe because I was there.

After I was married, my husband, David, and Susan and I decided to make a trip to Greensboro so that David could meet Miss Lady and Henretta. Judge had passed on two years earlier. David and I had been married in New York City, his hometown, and Judge and Miss Lady were unable to attend the wedding. We drove down in mid-February, which is early spring in Greensboro. Susan reminded us to make a fuss over the crocus, snowdrops, and winter jasmine in Henretta's garden. "And of course," she added, "we must remember to make a fuss over Miss Lady."

Miss Lady and Henretta were taken with David and tried to outdo each other in charming him. Miss Lady told him that she looked forward to reading his thesis on Rimbaud, and that she would be on the lookout for a good translation of his poems (Susan rolled her eyes at the prospect of Miss Lady reading Rimbaud). And when Henretta found out that February 17 was David's birthday, she immediately set about planning his birthday supper.

David and I returned to Miss Lady's house that afternoon to find the kitchen in an uproar. It seemed to be the usual commotion preceding a birthday celebration, until I realized that something was wrong. Susan's face was flushed and angry, and Henretta was wringing her hands.

"What's the matter?"

"Miss Lady has eaten a piece of David's birthday cake," said Susan.

"But that's impossible," I said. "The supper isn't until this evening."

"That's what I mean," said Susan. "Miss Lady helped herself before David even had a chance to see his cake, much less cut it."

Henretta struggled to be loyal to both Susan and Miss Lady. "I made the cake this morning," she said hesitantly. "I unmolded it and left it on the table and went out to work in the yard. It must have been about an hour ago. Miss Lady came in and cut herself a piece." She shook her head. "That Miss Lady is somethin' else."

I knew that the whiskey cake, rich and uniced, was a lot of trouble to make and so delicate it must be cut slowly and carefully with a saw-edged knife. It was baked in the shape of a loaf, and now one end was slightly ragged where Miss Lady had cut her piece.

"Where is Miss Lady now?" I asked.

"Taking her nap. Sleeping peacefully." Susan was triumphant. She seemed to be saying, "I'm right, I'm right! Everything I've always said about Miss Lady is true."

David and I noticed Henretta's distress. We took Susan into the backyard, out of Henretta's hearing.

"I'm embarrassed for her," I said.

"How could she have done it?" said Susan.

"Your grandmother is a great lady," said David.

"She is not!" said Susan. "She thinks she owns everything!"

"She's nervous, she's unhappy," I said. "Mamma says she's been that way ever since Judge died. She keeps hoping for something—anything—even a very small thing—that will make her happy, even for a few minutes. That will make her forget."

"You can say what you like," Susan retorted. "I say she's selfish."

"Let's pretend we don't know she did it," I suggested, "so David's birthday supper won't be ruined."

Grudgingly, Susan agreed.

The three hours that passed until supper was served were long enough to change the atmosphere in the house. Susan had time to take a nap, bathe, and put on a dress I had brought her from Paris. She came downstairs looking as if she had never, in all her life, been angry.

Miss Lady came to the table wearing her diamond brooch; she seemed blissfully unguilty. All during supper she and Susan vied for David's attention. It would be difficult to say who won. Susan had youth and beauty, but Miss Lady had Henretta in the kitchen.

David acquitted himself well of serving the cake by cutting at the *other* end. When Henretta served the lemon ice cream he said, "Food like this is not merely a means to life, but an end of life." Miss Lady liked this young man who knew how to pay a compliment. David, a vigorous Northeasterner, seemed delighted by this world where pleasure and charm were so important.

After supper, all of us, except Miss Lady, went back to the kitchen to thank Henretta. She wanted to know if Mr. David had enjoyed his birthday dinner.

"The best I've ever eaten," said David.

"And David has lived in Paris," said Susan, smoothing an imaginary wrinkle in her Paris dress and giving us her most dazzling smile.

Henretta was beaming with pleasure and pride.

Later, when we were alone, I asked David what he really thought of Southern food. He laughed and said, "It's so good it's sinful. Now I know why the South lost the Civil War."

Menu XI:

The supper that won David over to our side.

Tomato Soup

Beef Tenderloin, Onion, and Cheese Pie

Sunny Asparagus

Whiskey Cake

Penny's Lemon Ice Cream

Tomato Soup

A good way to use up those excess tomatoes at the end of summer.

> 12 ripe medium tomatoes (10 large), peeled and
>   chopped (retain juice)
> 1 cup water
> 1 tablespoon sugar
> 1 teaspoon salt
> 1/2 teaspoon pepper
> 1/4 teaspoon ground cloves
> 2 bay leaves
> 2 tablespoons butter
> 2 shallots, minced
> 1 tablespoon chopped fresh parsley
> 1 tablespoon flour
> 1/4 teaspoon baking soda

1. Put prepared tomatoes, water, sugar, salt, pepper, cloves, and bay leaves in a large pot and bring to boil; reduce heat and simmer 1 1/2 hours; remove bay leaves.

2. Melt butter in a small saucepan over medium heat. Add shallots and parsley, and sauté for 5 minutes. Add flour and cook roux 3 minutes more.

3. Add this mixture to tomatoes. Puree in batches in a blender or food processor.

4. Before serving, add baking soda, taste for seasoning, and simmer 10 minutes. Serve hot.

8 servings

Beef Tenderloin, Onion, and Cheese Pie

This also makes a nice entrée for a summer luncheon.

For the Pie Crust:

1 cup flour
1 stick butter
⅔ cup grated sharp Cheddar cheese

For the Filling:

1 pound filet of beef
4 tablespoons butter
4 medium-size yellow onions, thinly sliced
salt
pepper

For the Sauce:

4 egg yolks
1 cup heavy cream
½ teaspoon salt
1 pinch cayenne pepper
1 teaspoon grated nutmeg

1. To make the crust, cut the butter into the flour with two knives or a pastry blender. Add the grated cheese. Make the pastry into a ball. Roll out a 10-inch circle on floured board. Line a 9-inch pie pan with the dough. Set aside until ready to fill.

2. To make the filling, preheat oven to 375°F. Cut the beef into small pieces. Sauté the beef in the butter in a large skillet. Remove the meat

and add the onions. Cook slowly over low heat until they are soft but not browned, about 15 minutes. Add the meat, and season with salt and pepper. While the onions cook, prepare the sauce.

3. To make the sauce, beat egg yolks in a heavy saucepan; beat in the cream. Cook over low heat, stirring constantly, until custard thickens. Add salt, cayenne pepper, and nutmeg.

4. Put the beef and onions into the pie crust and pour over the sauce. Cook in oven 40 to 45 minutes. Serve hot.

8 servings

Sunny Asparagus

*T*he hard-boiled eggs add a subtle contrast in texture to the asparagus. For the best flavor, remove asparagus from cooking water before it turns dark green.

2 pounds asparagus, trimmed of tough bottom ends	pepper
salt	2 tablespoons butter, melted
	3 hard-boiled eggs, riced

1. In a large skillet, cover asparagus with cold water, bring to boil, reduce heat, partially cover, and simmer for about 15–20 minutes, or until tender but firm.

2. Drain and arrange on heated platter. Salt and pepper to taste, and pour melted butter over. Sprinkle hard-boiled eggs over top of asparagus. Serve immediately.

8 servings

Whiskey Cake

Good enough to steal a piece from *before* dessert.

1½ cups flour, divided
1 pound pecans, coarsely chopped
½ pound golden seedless raisins, halved
1 teaspoon baking powder
1 stick butter

1 cup plus 2 tablespoons sugar
3 eggs, separated
2 teaspoons freshly grated nutmeg
½ cup bourbon whiskey
pinch of salt

1. Preheat oven to 325°F.

2. Measure the flour after sifting once; then sift once more.

3. In a medium bowl, take ½ cup of the sifted flour and mix with raisins and nuts.

4. In a medium bowl, mix the rest of the flour with the baking powder and sift again.

5. In a large bowl, with an electric mixer, cream butter and sugar; add egg yolks one at a time, beating until mixture is smooth and lemon-colored.

6. Soak the freshly grated nutmeg in the bourbon whiskey for at least 10 minutes, then add whiskey to the butter and egg mixture, alternating with the cup of flour and beating as the batter is blended. Slowly fold the raisins and nuts into the batter.

7. Beat the egg whites with a pinch of salt until stiff, and fold delicately into the batter.

8. Butter a deep 10-inch metal tube pan or 2 large loaf pans. Fill the pans with the batter and let stand 10 minutes before putting into the oven.

9. Bake in oven for 75 minutes; if the top is browning too much, cover with a piece of foil. Cake should be slightly moist (be careful not to overcook); a few crumbs may adhere to the toothpick when it is inserted in center of cake. Let the cake stand in the pan for 30 minutes before trying to remove it.

10. To unmold, loosen delicately, then turn upside-down on a plate. Slice with a saw-edged knife, as it crumbles easily. This cake keeps well, and it cuts more easily if refrigerated.

16 servings

Penny's Lemon Ice Cream

A wonderful light rich "cream" (Henretta and Miss Lady's word for ice cream). And easy to make.

> 4 cups sugar
> grated rind of 1 large lemon
> 1 cup lemon juice (8–10 lemons)
> 1 quart heavy cream
> 1 quart light cream (half and half)
> 1 pint milk
> 4 teaspoons vanilla extract

1. Put sugar in a large bowl; mash in grated lemon peel. Add lemon juice, and stir to dissolve sugar. Add heavy cream, half and half, milk, and vanilla. Stir well.

2. Freeze in an ice-cream freezer according to manufacturer's directions.

2 quarts

Index

Susan (sister), 3, 7, 10, 12, 13, 14,
    19–21, 41–48, 60–61, 72,
    102–103, 104, 119–27, 137,
    138, 139, 164, 199–210
    photograph of, 18, 70, 198
Sweetbreads Salad, Chilled,
    82–83
Sweet Potatoes with Bourbon Sauce,
    193

Tart, Caviar, 89
Tennessee Jam Cake with Caramel
    Icing, 196–97
    story about, 180–88
Tomato(es):
    Aspic, 92
    with Caviar, 81
    Chicken with, and Avocados,
      131–32
    Green, Chutney, 113
    Soup, 212
    Stewed, 67
Trifle, 135
Turkey:
    with Chaudfroid Sauce, Galan-
      tine of, 78–80
    Roast, with Pecan Dressing,
      191–92

Veal:
    Loin of, Stuffed, 159–60
    Pheasant, Aunt Virginia's Terrine
      of, 87–88
    Turkey with Chaudfroid Sauce,
      Galantine of, 78–80
Vegetables, *see specific types of vegetables*
Vermouth with Walnuts and Green
    Grapes, Cousin Catherine's,
    145–46
Virginia, Aunt, 12–13, 15, 16, 24,
    47, 101, 102, 103
    photograph of, xii

Watermelon Rind Pickle, 93
Whiskey, bourbon, *see* Bourbon
    Whiskey
William (grandson of Miss Annie),
    21–22, 72
World War II, 12, 101, 105

Yeast Rolls, Cousin Catherine's
    Potato, 195

Zucchini with Nutmeg, 174